CRAVE
VANCOUVER

The Urban Girl's Manifesto

Melody Biringer

the urban girl

manifes

The Urban Girl's Manifesto

We CRAVE Community.
At CRAVE Vancouver we believe in acknowledging, celebrating, and passionately supporting local businesses. We know that, when encouraged to thrive, neighbourhood establishments enhance communities and provide rich experiences not usually encountered in mass-market. By introducing you to the savvy businesswomen in this guide, we hope that CRAVE Vancouver will help inspire your own inner entrepreneur.

We CRAVE Adventure.
We could all use a getaway, and at CRAVE Vancouver we believe that you don't need to be a jet-setter to have a little adventure. There's so much to do and explore right in your own backyard. We encourage you to break your routine, to venture away from your regular haunts, to visit new businesses, to explore all the funky finds and surprising spots that Vancouver has to offer. Whether it's to hunt for a birthday gift, indulge in a spa treatment, order a bouquet of flowers, or connect with like-minded people, let CRAVE Vancouver be your guide for a one-of-a-kind hometown adventure.

We CRAVE Quality.
CRAVE Vancouver is all about quality products and thoughtful service. We know that a satisfying shopping trip requires more than a simple exchange of money for goods, and that a rejuvenating spa date entails more than a quick clip of the cuticles and a swipe of polish. We know you want to come away feeling uplifted, beautiful, excited, relaxed, relieved and, above all, knowing you got the most bang for your buck. We have scoured the city to find the hidden gems, new hot spots, and old standbys, all with one thing in common: they're the best of the best!

A Guide to Our Guide

CRAVE Vancouver is more than a guidebook. It's a savvy, quality-of-lifestyle book devoted entirely to the best local businesses owned by women. CRAVE Vancouver will direct you to more than 150 local spots—top boutiques, spas, cafés, stylists, fitness studios, and more. And we'll introduce you to the inspired, dedicated women behind these exceptional enterprises, for whom creativity, quality, innovation, and customer service are paramount.

Not only is CRAVE Vancouver an intelligent guidebook for those wanting to know what's happening throughout town, it's a directory for those who value the contributions that spirited businesswomen make to our city.

Icon Key

Featured Entreprenesses

 Abode Furniture, home improvement and interior design

 Adorn Jewellery, eyewear, handbags and accessories

 Connect Networking, media, technology and event services

 Details Gifts, books, small home accessories, florists and stationery

 Enhance Beauty, wellness, spas and fitness

 Escape Entertainment, travel and leisure activities

 Nurture Goods and services for babies, children and parents

 Pets Goods and services for pets and their owners

 Sip Savour Food and drink

 Style Clothing, shoes and stylists

Intelligentsia

 Coach Coaches and consultants

 Communicate Marketing, PR and branding strategy

 Create Graphic and web design and media services

 Entertain Event services

 Finance Accountants and money management specialists

 Law Law offices and attorneys

 Network Networking events, programs and social media

 Real Estate Real estate, property management and moving services

 Staff Staffing agencies and recruiters

 Support Organization services and personal assistants

 Tech Technology support

Additional

 Nonprofit Not-for-profit business

 Discount Offers a discount in Craving Savings

 Sustainable Devoted to environmentally friendly practices

Table of Contents

featured
entrepre

Featured Entreprenesses

*Including retailers, restaurants,
fitness studios, fashion designers,
online retailers, event planners, home
accessories, pet stores, lifestyle
and wellness-related products,
travel services, spas and salons.*

18KARAT

3039 Granville St, Vancouver, 604.742.1880
eighteenkarat.com

Modern. Global. Nature-inspired.
18KARAT is an international brand of home decor and furnishings. The store in the South Granville neighbourhood is an exciting test site for new products and ideas. New collections are launched regularly—always inspired by stories from the natural world, interpreted in a modern way. Don't miss the garden in the alley.

Q&A

Maureen Welton

What are your most popular
products or services?
Architect-designed furniture, home and
garden accessories, and design books.

What tip would you give women
who are starting a business?
Love what you do. Do it honestly,
invest all your passion and don't expect
anything in return. Success will come
in its own way—it can't be forced.

What is your favourite part about
owning a small business?
The ability to manage my own life, even when
it feels unmanageable. Travelling to amazing
places for my job, meeting and working
with really cool people around the world.

What do you CRAVE?
Brilliantly simple, beautiful solutions whether
they're in food, clothing, home or conversation.

Jennifer Scott and
Rachel Harrison

 Q&A

What is your favourite part about
owning a small business?
New challenges and opportunities that come
with owning a small business allow us to learn,
grow and gain confidence, while the nature of
our outfit provides a strong creative outlet.

What motivates you on a daily basis?
Our daughters. We want our girls to grow up
knowing that success doesn't have a price,
style doesn't compromise, confidence is beauty
and compassionate women can have it all.

What is your motto or theme song?
Style is merely a blend of confidence,
design principles and fun. Everyone can
achieve it. We can show you how.

How do you relax?
Yoga, family time, the beach, running,
alone time, laughter, a great glass
of *vino*. And, yes, shopping.

A GOOD CHICK TO KNOW DESIGN CONSULTATION

778.228.9222, 778.837.4559
agoodchicktoknow.com, Twitter: @goodchicktoknow

Fresh. Polished. Fashion-forward.
Fabulous style has no limit. A Good Chick To Know Design Consultation works with you to develop your own personal sense of design for your home decor and wardrobe, and teaches to you to translate that into your daily life with confidence. With a keen and well-versed sense of style, the Chicks can help you shape up the chic and ship out the shabby!

Photos by Bopomo Pictures

Q&A

Suzanne Fetting

What tip would you give women
who are starting a business?
Believe in yourself! Confidence is the most
important component when starting a business.
You *must* believe in yourself and your abilities,
because if you don't, no one else will!

What is your favourite part about
owning a small business?
I love the fact that I look forward to
working each day and I love the freedom
of having a flexible schedule.

What motivates you on a daily basis?
Seeing the transformations that take
place in my clients and students is
incredibly motivating and rewarding.

What do you CRAVE?
Shoes, shoes and more shoes!

ABSOLUTE CONFIDENCE

604.230.5538
absoluteconfidence.com, Twitter: @absolutecoach

Empowering. Results-driven. Rewarding.
Absolute Confidence aims to empower women of all ages, shapes and sizes by assisting them in discovering their authentic selves and learning how to trust and love themselves more.

HIGH HEEL APPEAL

highheelappeal.com

Fun. Informative. Unique.
The High Heel Appeal class and instructional DVD teaches women how to boost their confidence—and their height—with a pair of high heels.

15

ABSOLUTE SPA GROUP

Located at Century, Fairmont Hotel Vancouver, Fairmont Vancouver Airport, YVR, River Rock Casino Resort and Park Royal South, 604.684.2772
absolutespa.com, Twitter: @absolutespa

Luxurious. Affordable. Award-winning.
In 11 years, Wendy Lisogar-Cocchia has grown her business from one location at the flagship Century Plaza Hotel to 11 Absolute Spas, becoming Canada's largest and most luxurious spa chain. These world-class spas have been voted and awarded "best spa" more than 50 times by publications such as *The Georgia Straight, Vancouver Magazine*, *Vancouver Courier, Glow Magazine*, Vancouver's *Best Places Magazine*, *Prestige Magazine*, and more. As a leader in the beauty, health and wellness industry, Absolute Spa is *the* choice for celebrities.

Main photo (this page) and upper right and middle photos (opposite page) by Melissa Gidney Photography, upper left photo by Absolute Spa

Wendy Lisogar-Cocchia

 Q&A

What tip would you give women who are starting a business?
Choose an industry you love; awake every morning with excitement and enthusiasm. Never, ever give up; persevere. Believe in your yourself and always pursue your dreams.

What is your favourite part about owning a business?
I love contributing to the community by volunteering with organisations such as the Vancouver Board of Trade, Vancouver Police Foundation or BC's Special Children's Charities.

How do you relax?
Spending quality time with family and friends and, of course, a visit to the spa with them in one of our VIP suites.

Izabela Sauer

 # Q&A

Who is your role model or mentor?
Sonia Delaunay, an early 20th-century French painter, printmaker, textile designer and interior decorator—a true renaissance woman who ran her various enterprises well into her 90s.

What is your motto or theme song?
Smile mysteriously and let them wonder what you are smiling about.

How do you relax?
I love being in the ocean: sailing, swimming or diving. I think I was a mermaid in a previous life.

What place inspires you and why?
The South Pacific islands are the most inspiring to me for their bright colours and smiles of Polynesians.

What do you CRAVE?
Beauty in every aspect of my life.

ALARTE SILKS

1369 Railspur Alley, Vancouver, 778.370.4304
alartesilks.com

Colourful. Glamourous. Sophisticated.
Alarte Silks specialises in one-of-a-kind hand-painted silks represented by fine craft galleries throughout North America. Owner Izabela Sauer creates unique hand-felted wools and hand-painted and hand-pleated silks—from delicate chiffons to luminous jacquards—that showcase an exceptional gift for detail and artistic expression. Exotic colourations invoke a Mediterranean sky, a shock of bougainvillea or deep verdant greens. Her work embodies contemporary styling and a true vision of personal adornment.

Photos by Go-Lucky Photography

Candice Albach

Q&A

What is your favourite part about owning a small business?
The best part of owning a small business is the interaction I get to have with so many interesting people. Also, I love that the possibilities are endless.

Who is your role model or mentor?
Janie Hewson, owner of Marketing Creatives. She started out as a marketing teacher in California, then became my marketing consultant and now friend. She is bluntly honest and so very caring.

What place inspires you and why?
I am inspired everywhere! Seriously. In my opinion the world is a giant set and there is always something that makes me want to make a picture.

☎ ALBACH STUDIOS

888.456.7448
albachstudios.com, Twitter: @ALBACHfoto

Dynamic. Sensitive. Passionate.
Newly relocated to Vancouver, Albach Studios provides photography services specialising in people, products and food. Because there are no templates, text-book lighting schemes or studio backdrops (unless requested), Albach Studios creates authentic and original images. Albach Studios embraces spontaneity, resulting in pictures that convey true moments, character and relationships.

BABS STUDIO BOUTIQUE

2410 Granville St S, Vancouver, 604.408.4881
babs.ca

Artistic. Stylish. Forever.
Babs Studio Boutique is a very rare and special place where women can feel like women. Catering to all shapes and sizes (2–26), designs are extremely well-fitting, unique, and high-quality. The boutique also carries five other Canadian labels to die for, along with in-store tailoring, making sure the clothes you buy fit you perfectly.

Babs Lucas

Q&A

What are your most popular products or services?
Our primary focus is fit! After that, we specifically dress women in the style and shape for their personal needs. Women can work in Babs, travel in Babs, dine in Babs, go to a wedding in Babs, get the job and keep it in Babs, and simply get noticed in Babs.

Who is your role model or mentor?
Vivienne Westwood.

What is your motto or theme song?
Innovate or die.

What place inspires you and why?
My work encourages me to travel internationally in search of beautiful textiles. Whether I am in Cambodia, Japan, France or right here on the West Coast, I feel very, very lucky.

Aiyana Kane and Jackie Avery

Q&A

What are your most popular
products or services?
Tacos, soups, salads, enchiladas,
brunch, local beer and wine, fresh and
interesting house-made cocktails and
rich vegan chocolate brownies.

What is your favourite part about
owning a small business?
The freedom to make our own choices,
solve problems in creative ways and put
staff and our business philosophy first.

What motivates you on a daily basis?
Creating a space that promotes wellness for
our staff, customers, community and planet.

What place inspires you and why?
Little Nest and Radha: two restaurants
in Vancouver that serve beautiful
food and are committed to the
community and the environment.

BANDIDAS TAQUERÍA

2781 Commercial Drive, Vancouver, 604.568.8224
bandidastaqueria.com

Fresh. Vegetarian. Warm.
Bandidas Taquería is a great little restaurant on Vancouver's Commercial Drive. The menu is Mexican-inspired and original in that it is all vegetarian and can be ordered vegan. Everything is made fresh daily: hand-cut salsa, rich and complex mole, hand-pressed corn tortillas. Bandidas serves breakfast, lunch and dinner daily, offering a full bar with local beer and wine and an original, fresh cocktail menu.

Photos by Jordana Dhahan of Through the Looking Glass Photography

THE BAR METHOD

837 Beatty St, Ste 201, Vancouver, 604.681.6188
vancouver.barmethod.com, Twitter: @barmethod_van

Strong. Flexible. Friendly.
The Bar Method is a one-hour core-strengthening exercise program, combining yoga, Pilates and ballet to lengthen, strengthen and sculpt the body. The Bar Method provides a targeted workout, which includes fat-burning interval training, muscle-shaping isometrics, ballet conditioning and physical therapy to quickly sculpt the entire physique. Muscles look longer and more defined, and the body becomes leaner and more slender.

Main photo (this page) by Kari Heese, portrait by Melissa Gidney Photography

Carolyn Williams

 Q&A

What tip would you give women
who are starting a business?
As soon as you have realized
something isn't working, change it.

What is your favourite part about
owning a small business?
All the incredible people I have met along the
way. I feel so fortunate to be in a business where
I constantly meet new and interesting people.

Who is your role model or mentor?
My dad has been one of my mentors. The years
of watching my dad run his own businesses
has led me up to this point in life; I am excited.

What place inspires you and why?
At the start of a race, I always get
emotional as I look around and see excited
people who have trained so hard.

Eva de Viveiros

Q&A

What is your favourite part about owning a small business?
So many things! I get to share my passion and creativity every day—to hunt for and display my treasures and see how they delight and inspire others.

Who is your role model or mentor?
My mother. Incredibly hard working and creative, she could make anything with those fabulously talented hands.

What is your motto or theme song?
A man had wandered in, looked around and asked, "What is this place?" Before I could answer, a customer turned around and said, "Why, all things lovely!" It stuck.

What do you CRAVE?
More time to create... and a bigger studio!

I am not interested in money, I just want to be wonderful
- Marilyn Monroe

Photos by Candice Albach

BAREFOOT CONTESSA

3715 Main St, Vancouver, 604.879.1137 x1
1928 Commercial Drive, Vancouver, 604.255.9035 x2
thebarefootcontessa.com, barefootcontessaliving.blogspot.com, Twitter: @so_lovely

Feminine. Whimsical. Vintage-inspired.
Barefoot Contessa is a delightful purveyor of gorgeous clothing and covet-worthy jewellery. From the sublime to the mundane, everything is picked with an eye for detail—luxurious or whimsical. Picket-fence changing rooms, charming staff and an attention to detail make shopping fun again. Guilty pleasure, beloved secret... Barefoot Contessa is a jewel box of fabulous!

29

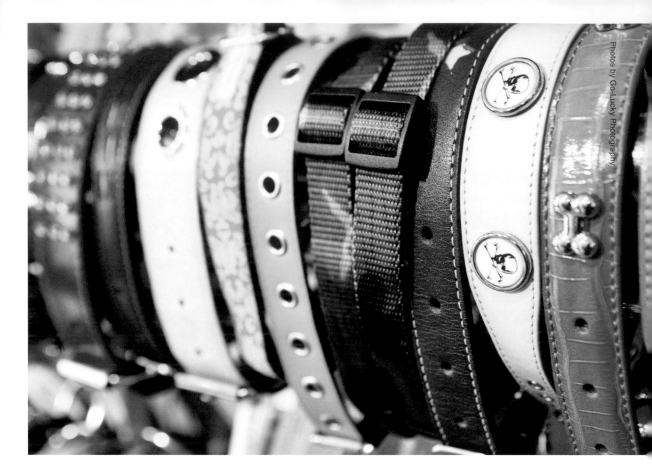

Photos by Go-Lucky Photography

BARKING BABIES

1188 Homer St, Vancouver, 604.647.BARK (2275)
barkingbabies.com, Twitter: @barking_babies

Fun. Vibrant. Chic.
The concept of barking babies is simple—they recognize the importance of your barking baby and strive to enhance their lifestyle by offering fashionably hip, urban goods that are well-designed, functional and fun. After all... barking babies deserve the best!

Nancy Jelenic

Q&A

What are your most popular products or services?
Stylish dog carriers to sneak and tote your "babies," cashmere dog sweaters, tweed dog trench coats, Swarovski collars with matching leashes and doggie spa products.

What tip would you give women who are starting a business?
Really research the location. Yaletown is filled with small dogs—I would have only opened my boutique here.

How do you relax?
A glass of white wine, cooking, gardening, hot yoga and meeting with friends.

What place inspires you and why?
Kyoto and Tokyo. The juxtaposition between the two cities is awe-inspiring; the culture still holds onto its roots so strongly. And Tokyo has the best dog fashion anywhere!

Yaletown

Shauna Magrath

Q&A

What are your most popular products or services?
By far our permanent cosmetics... Eyebrows to be more specific. Everyone wants to have amazing brows without all the effort and after all, why wouldn't you?

What tip would you give women who are starting a business?
Do your research! Don't lose sight of your dream. Remember to honor the "knowing" that drives you each and every day! Utilize the services available, i.e., the Women's Enterprise Center.

How do you relax?
Spending time at the beach, enjoying a day at the spa, cooking an incredible gourmet meal or traveling on a wild adventure.

BEAUTYINK GALLERY

101-1529 W Sixth Ave, Vancouver 604.639.3609
beautyink.ca, Twitter: @BeautyInk

Compassionate. Elite. Tranquil.
BeautyInk Gallery is Vancouver's first exclusive makeup service boutique
specialising in permanent cosmetics and custom creations for ladies or
gentlemen. Their passion is working with cancer, burn and accident survivors,
but they also love creating alluring looks for your specific makeup needs.
With personal lessons for special occasions, brows, liner, lashes or a new
you, the BeautyInk Gallery will define your elegance for years to come!

Mimie Lee

Q&A

What are your most popular
products or services?
A unique gift for parents, grandparents,
teachers and friends *created by you!*

What is your favourite part about
owning a small business?
Meeting many interesting people and
making friends with my customers.

Who is your role model or mentor?
Leonardo da Vinci. What a genius.
Where would we be without him?

How do you relax?
Painting ceramics! Whenever I am stressed,
I just paint. Ceramic painting is cheaper
than therapy and a lot more fun.

What place inspires you and why?
The ocean with no land in sight.
It gives me peace.

BELLA CERAMICA

1381 Marine Drive, 2nd Floor, West Vancouver, 604.925.3115
bellaceramicastudio.com

Creative. Therapeutic. Educational.
With close to 2,000 square feet of open floor space and a spectacular view of
the water, Bella Ceramica is one of the best art studios to get your creative juices
flowing. The fabulous studio offers ceramic painting, mosaic, glass-fusing and
clay workshops. It is a popular place for kids' parties, wedding showers, corporate
parties or a girls' night out! With no reservation required, drop in anytime!

West Vancouver

Photos by Go-Lucky Photography

BELMONDO
ORGANIC SKIN CARE

belmondo.ca, Twitter: @danielabelmondo

Nourishing. Healing. Ethical.
Belmondo reminds us to take part in the daily ritual of caring for yourself. This
natural skin care line brims with earth-grown goodness that your body recognizes
and uses to heal and beautify itself. All products are made in small batches,
produced locally, and product testing is done only on willing two-legged friends,
never on animals. Check them out online and at selected retail locations.

Photos by Candice Albach

Daniela Belmondo

 Q&A

What are your most popular
products or services?
I have two top sellers: The Rain, a gentle,
invigorating face cleanser, and The Cloud,
a smoothing, velvety face cream.

What tip would you give women
who are starting a business?
A wise mentor recently shared with me her
great philosophy: "Correct and continue."

What motivates you on a daily basis?
Customer feedback. When I know a product
has had an impact on someone and I've made
a difference, there is no better motivator.

What place inspires you and why?
The world. There is so much greatness
happening every day and we have a
lot to learn from one another. It's an
inspiring and beautiful place to be.

BLOOM ESSENTIALS

3-1854 W First Ave, Vancouver, 604.736.8960
bloomessentials.com

BUG & PICKLE

bugandpickle.com

Knowledgeable. Friendly. Fun.
Sisters Kim and Nicole made their first mark on the business world as little girls selling corn from their wagon. Later, they opened Bloom Essentials, a welcoming spa that offers a knowledgeable staff with a passion for over-the-top customer service and back-to-basics treatments. Their success in the beauty industry has led to the launch of Bug & Pickle, a whimsical line of body products for mums and babes.

Kimberly and Nicole Critten

 # Q&A

What are your most popular
products or services?
Our Picasso Pedicure put us on the map
and 13 years later it is still going strong.
We can do anything from perfectly painted
daisies to sparkly zebra stripes.

What is your favourite part about
owning a small business?
Knowing that we built a successful business
from scratch at a very young age.

Who is your role model or mentor?
Our parents have played a huge role
in our success: they taught us to work
hard when we were just little.

How do you relax?
Spending time with our family... and trashy TV!

What do you CRAVE?
We crave time to do everything we
would like to do... and cupcakes!

Kitsilano

bug & pickle
FOR MUMS & BABES

BABY BUTTER
•
CRÈME POUR BÉBÉ

Soothe baby's sensitive or extra-dry skin w
this buttery balm enriched with lavender,
chamomile & orange.

NET WT. 2 OZ. (57 g)

BLUE RUBY JEWELLERY

1085 Robson St, Vancouver, 604.899.2583
Hills of Kerrisdale: 2125 W 41st Ave, Vancouver, 604.266.9177
Oakridge Centre: 650 W 41st Ave, Vancouver, 604.269.2583
Pacific Centre: 701 W Georgia St, Vancouver, 604.693.3118
Park Royal: 945 Park Royal S, West Vancouver, 604.913.3118
Metropolis at Metrotown: 4700 Kingsway, Burnaby 604.454.9334
Richmond Centre: 6551 No 3 Road, Richmond, 604.247.2583
blueruby.com

Luxurious. Timeless. Glamourous.
Blue Ruby is an original jewellery boutique showcasing designers from
around the world and from the pages of fashion magazines. With seven
luxurious retail locations throughout Vancouver and surrounding areas, Blue
Ruby represents beauty, style and individuality. A visit to Blue Ruby inspires
every customer to seize the moment and transform their personal style.

Nancy Hill

 Q&A

What tip would you give women who are starting a business?
Stick to your guns and don't let anyone discourage you.

What is your favourite part about owning a small business?
When people tell me how much they love my stores.

Who is your role model or mentor?
My mom and dad. Both are very hardworking and practical.

What is your biggest fear?
Boredom.

What place inspires you and why?
My cabin. It's a very peaceful and beautiful place.

West End

West Vancouver

Downtown

Burnaby

Kerrisdale

Kim Anami

Q&A

What are your most popular products or services?
Packages that feature life or intimacy coaching sessions combined with your pick of a Sexual Savant Salon like The Multi-Orgasmic Couple or The Art of Pleasuring a Man.

Who is your role model or mentor?
Anyone who has the courage to go against the grain, speak her mind and live the unique life that is her gift to the world.

What do you CRAVE?
Passionate, soulful people. Intimacy. Spiritual connection. Innovation and creativity. Beauty. Sunshine. Witty banter. Getting off the grid and into nature. Surfing. Sex!

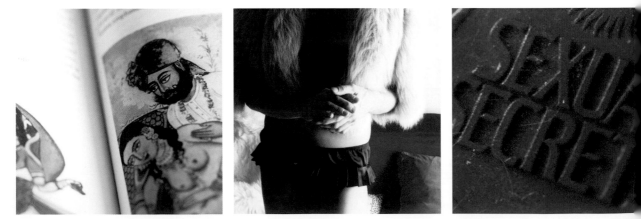

BODACIOUS LIFE AND SEX COACHING

604.602.8100
bodaciouslifecoaching.com, Twitter: @KimAnami

Bold. Innovative. Inspiring.
Kim Anami is a life, sex and relationship coach inspiring you to manifest the most vibrant and fulfilling life you can imagine. Believing sexual energy to be a powerful source of creativity and pleasure, she coaches privately and in groups to help people reclaim their passion and juice. She has been featured in *Flare*, on national television and radio, and she's written for *Playboy* magazine.

Lorna Ketler and Barb Wilkins

Q&A

What are your most popular products or services?
Wrap dresses, bamboo casual wear and leggings.

What tip would you give women who are starting a business?
Get a good accountant. Pay the professionals to do what they do best and take advice on growth planning, budgeting, etc. Have fun and listen to your customer.

What motivates you on a daily basis?
Our customers. A happy customer who tells us and others about a positive shopping experience is the best motivator!

What is your motto or theme song?
Celebrate Your Curves!

BODACIOUS LIFESTYLES INC.

4393 Main St, Vancouver, 604.874.2811
Molly's Lane Market, Gibsons, 604.970.4393
bodacious.ca, Twitter: @bodaciouslife

Celebratory. Curvy. Welcoming.
When you open the pretty pink doors of Bodacious, you know you're in
for a fun and supportive shopping experience. Featuring sizes 10–24 and
funky, stylin' fashion, co-owners Lorna and Barb have chosen a wide range
of designs with a focus on local. Buttery-soft bamboo casual wear, figure-
flattering dresses, wide-calf boots, fabulous accessories and so much more!

b·dacious
sizes 10-24... cothing to celebrate your curves

clothing to celebrate your curves

Photos by Jordana Dhahan of Through the Looking Glass Photography

Photos by Jordana Dhahan of Through the Looking Glass Photography

BODY POLITIC

208 E 12th Ave, Vancouver, 604.568.5528
bodypolitic.ca, Twitter: @body_politic

Meaningful. Chic. Engaging.
With a quick step around the corner of Vancouver's vibrant Main Street, you'll find body politic. The simple storefront belies the innovative and chic eco-designers from Vancouver to New York that are showcased within. "Sustainable design, limitless style" is the mandate of body politic and each collection is chosen for its sustainability story as well as edited for an urban style aesthetic. Granola? Only for breakfast!

Q&A

Nicole
Ritchie-Oseen

What tip would you give women
who are starting a business?
Be brave, trust in your abilities and
build a team around you that excels
in different areas in which you'll need
help. These people are invaluable!

What is your favourite part about
owning a small business?
Meeting like-minded people every day
who embrace body politic is a thrill.

What motivates you on a daily basis?
Knowing that there is vast room for growth
in this area of the industry and many more
people to be reached. Creating change
through body politic keeps me interested.

What is your motto or theme song?
Hakuna Matata! You just can't
be serious all of the time.

Zuka Artful Accessories photographed
by Go-Lucky Photography

What tip would you give women
who are starting a business?

" *Don't talk yourself out of
what you're meant to do.* "

Jordan Tomas Proulx of Pebble

Ravy Mehroke and Amy Minhas

Q&A

What is your favourite part about owning a small business?
Everything! We love being our own boss, being empowered businesswomen with a big vision and building a brow-obsessed community. Most importantly, we love making our clients look and feel beautiful!

Who is your role model or mentor?
Our business advisor and mentor, Judy Brooks, co-founder of Blo Blow Dry Bar. She has provided us with the courage, knowledge and insights to run a successful business, bar none!

What is your biggest fear?
No fear. We're super-calculated risk takers who always try our best to move forward with courage and poise. We plan and then execute... all with perfect brows!

rock your brows.
indian style.

BOMBAY BROW BAR

1056 Mainland St, Vancouver, 604.683.2769
bombaybrowbar.com, Twitter: @bombaybrowbar

Vibrant. Girly. Fun.
Battle the brows no more and rock out in Bombay princess-style.
Bombay is not a spa. They have a major brow obsession—it's all they
do. For 23 dollars, pick a shaping technique and leave with perfectly
sculpted brows in less than 20 minutes. No pain, no hassle. Just
serious brow perfection so you can rock your brows—Indian style!

Yaletown

BONN CHIROPRACTIC

3-1238 Homer St, Vancouver, 604.688.KIDS (5437)
bonnchiropractic.com

Natural. Integrative. Holistic.
Bonn Chiropractic is a practice focused on optimizing health and wellness naturally. Dr. Stephanie has an integrative and holistic approach incorporating exercise, nutrition advice and lifestyle recommendations with chiropractic care specific to the individual. She welcomes you to her office for help with issues such as ergonomic strain, prenatal stress, colicky newborns or children with pediatric headaches—for a chiropractic wellness lifestyle!

◾ Q&A

What is your favourite part about owning a small business?
The one-on-one connection with each individual, whether a client or networking contact. Flexibility with respect to having a family. The ability to run my business exactly the way I want to run it!

Who is your role model or mentor?
Dr. Jeanne Ohm, DC: family chiropractor, mother of six, executive editor of *Pathways* of the International Chiropractic Pediatric Association and renowned speaker for the ICPA Fellowship Program.

What motivates you on a daily basis?
The definition of chiropractic: the art of the physical adjustment, the science behind it and philosophy of our innate healing potential—it's more than just back pain relief!

Stephanie Bonn

bonn chiropractic inc.
FAMILY • HEALTH • WELLNESS

Dr. Stephanie Bonn
BSc, BPHE, DC

@ Yaletown Chiropractic
3-1238 H...

Yaletown

BOPOMO PICTURES

2631 W Broadway, Vancouver, 604.678.1411
The Shops at Morgan Crossing: 110-15745 Croydon Drive, Surrey, 778.294.0711
bopomo.ca, Twitter: @bopomopictures

Fresh. Irresistible. Inspired.
Bopomo Pictures combines fun, convenience and affordability with high-quality photography in a hip studio setting. Bopomo creates timeless memories with maternity, baby and family pictures, and helps professionals and businesses make a lasting impact with headshot and commercial photography. The studio also offers a range of unique retail items, including birth announcements, greeting cards, canvas prints and custom accessories such as jewelry and handbags.

Elayne Wandler

# Q&A

What are your most popular
products or services?
The value multi-pack allows clients to
customise a package of 20-plus prints and
add digital images for only $99.95. Also
extremely popular is our canvas print series.

What is your favourite part about
owning a small business?
The ability to create something from
the ground up is very exciting. It is
exhilarating to bring a concept to life and
have it embraced by consumers.

Who is your role model or mentor?
My father for his integrity, wisdom,
work ethic and sense of humor.

What is your motto or theme song?
Trust life and trust your instincts.

BOW WOW HAUS

1340 Davie St, Vancouver, 604.682.1899
1701 W Fourth Ave, Vancouver, 604.563.5009
bowwowhaus.ca, Twitter: @bowwowhaus

Chic. Modern. Friendly.
Bow wow haus is a go-to spot for modern dogs and their people for an
unrivaled selection of chic gear and healthy eats. Staffed by a team of friendly,
knowledgeable dog lovers, customers will find products that reflect their
commitment to the health, style, and well-being of their furry friends. From the
cutest party dresses to sturdy hiking packs, they have something for every dog!

Suji Moon

⧉ Q&A

What are your most popular
products or services?
A great selection of collars, toys and rain
jackets. Super-stylish carriers that comfortably
transport (and camouflage!) little canines.
A boutique daycare for small dogs that
provides expert care and much love.

What motivates you on a daily basis?
Owning my own business in itself is a huge
motivator. I wake up every day knowing
the effort I put in directly impacts the
success of my business—it's powerful.

How do you relax?
Unsurprisingly, I spend time with my dogs! We
live in a breathtakingly beautiful city and we take
full advantage of our mountains and oceans.

What do you CRAVE?
Happiness, good health, success and,
of course, lots of doggie smooches!

Brooke Mosher

Q&A

What are your most popular
products or services?
All of my hammered and brushed earrings,
necklaces and bracelets. My bridal collection
is growing every season and earrings are
always in demand from my customers.

What is your favourite part about
owning a small business?
Not having to answer to anybody else, and
since I work from home I can wear whatever I
want. I make the rules and I like it that way.

What is your motto or theme song?
"Don't worry about a thing, because every
little thing is gonna be alright."—Bob Marley.
I listen to this song because it keeps
me focussed and relaxed.

Brooklyn DESIGNS

Brooke Mosher
www.brooklyndesigns.ca
info@brooklyndesigns.ca
604-584-0808

Sterling Silver & 14 K Gold-Filled
Handcrafted Jewelry

BROOKLYN DESIGNS

778.228.4360
brooklyndesigns.ca, Twitter: @brklyndesigns

Modern. Versatile. Sophisticated.
Brooklyn Designs is a leading jewellery label. Finding inspiration from BC's South Coast, its understated glamour makes Brooklyn Designs the perfect choice for the everyday woman. Designer Brooke Mosher combines high-quality gemstones, Swarovski crystals, 14-karat. gold-filled and sterling silver components to create her in-demand jewellery. Each piece is handmade by Brooke, available online and across Canada.

BURKE&HAIR

508-55 Water St, Vancouver, 604.687.4247
burkeandhair.com, Twitter: @BurkeAndHair

Urban. Exclusive. Relaxed.
Burke&Hair is a neighbourhood gem. Tucked in a converted, historic loft, overlooking
the beautiful North Shore mountains and Burrard Inlet, this relaxed, exclusive salon
offers one-on-one, personalized hair services to Vancouver's discerning urbanites.
With more than 17 years of experience hairdressing in both the salon and for film
and television, owner Melanie Burke strives to create for you the "perfect hair love."

Photos by Melissa Gidney Photography

Melanie Burke

 # Q&A

What tip would you give women who are starting a business?
Call for backup! Whether it's financial support, emotional support or straight-talking business advice you need, find mentors and people excited about your business and collaborate with them!

What is your favourite part about owning a small business?
Giving my clients an experience I know I would like, everything from the espresso to the colour of the walls to the music playing. It's a sanctuary for all.

What is your motto or theme song?
"When you change the way you look at things, the things you look at change."—Wayne Dyer

What do you CRAVE?
The crispy grilled cheese with tomato soup at the Pourhouse! Yum!

Photos by Candice Albach, except portrait by Janis Nicolay

BUTTER BAKED GOODS

4321 Dunbar St, Vancouver, 604.221.4333
butterbakedgoods.com, Twitter: @butterbaking

Nostalgic. Yummy. Fun.
Butter Baked Goods is all about the treats you remember from childhood.
Nothing fancy. Just good old-fashioned cakes, cookies, bars and pies just like
Mom made. It has been three years since Butter opened the doors and they
haven't looked back since. Butter's line of gourmet marshmallows and s'mores
can be found in more than 200 gourmet grocery stores across North America.

Q&A

Rosie Daykin

What are your most popular products or services?
Marshmallows and the homemade You Know What (two chocolate cookies sandwiched around vanilla butter cream).

What tip would you give women who are starting a business?
Just go for it.

What is your favourite part about owning a small business?
Knowing all my customers so well. It is such a fantastic sense of community.

What motivates you on a daily basis?
Being a great role model for my 17-year-old daughter.

What place inspires you and why?
San Francisco. They have such a great food scene.

Caroline Calvert

Q&A

What are your most popular
products or services?
Bridal gowns, bridesmaids
dresses and birdcage veils.

What tip would you give women
who are starting a business?
Have a cash flow and update it weekly so
you know where your money is or isn't.

What is your motto or theme song?
The glass is half full, and "Sweet
Caroline"—I think that was a given.

What place inspires you and why?
Getting away from the city and the
daily grind inspires me to be creative,
preferably in a cabin near the ocean with
my family in a cozy blanket near a fire.

CAROLINE CALVERT COUTURE

3578 W Fourth Ave, Vancouver
carolinecalvert.com, Twitter: @carolinecalvert

Elegant. Well-designed. Chic.
Caroline Calvert's intimate boutique has a wide selection of her bridal
gowns and bridesmaid dresses that are designed and made in Vancouver.
If you can't find what you are looking for, they can design you a custom
gown. Caroline's boutique also carries a beautifully designed collection of
accessories, such as veils, garters, ring pillows, purses and jewelry.

Anne Rowland and
Lisa Zumpano

 Q&A

What are your most popular
products or services?
Equestrian supplies, outerwear, clothing,
boots, home decor and dog accessories.

What tip would you give women
who are starting a business?
Start small, be conservative, and let the
business evolve and grow gradually.

What motivates you on a daily basis?
Making people and horses
content and comfortable.

What is your motto or theme song?
The more you put in, the more you get back.

What place inspires you and why?
The English countryside.

THE CARRINGTON SHOPPE

3434 W 55th Ave, Vancouver, 604.266.5725
thecarringtonshoppe.com

Specialised. Country. Classic.
The Carrington Shoppe is a premier country lifestyle and tack boutique.
Located on the west side of Vancouver in the equestrian enclave of
Southlands, the shop is reminiscent of an English village store catering
to the local country clientele. Offering products for the horse, the home,
the rider and non-rider alike, this store epitomizes country elegance.

Photos by Jordana Dhahan of Through the Looking Glass Photography,
except photo (this page) by Aimee Makris for Moi Photography

Dunbar-Southlands

CHAMBAR RESTAURANT

562 Beatty St, Vancouver, 604.879.7119
chambar.com, Twitter: @chambar

CAFÉ MEDINA

556 Beatty St, Vancouver, 604.879.3114
medinacafe.com, Twitter: @cafemedina

THE DIRTY APRON COOKING SCHOOL

540 Beatty St, Vancouver , 604.879.8588
dirtyapron.com, Twitter: @dirty_apron

Unpretentious. Vibrant. Original.
Chambar offers Belgian-themed food with North African influence paired with stunning cocktails, an extensive Belgian beer list and an inventive selection of affordable wines. Next door, Café Medina serves Belgian waffles for sweet sustenance and offers an eclectic alternative for breakfast, brunch and lunch. Down the street, The Dirty Apron Cooking School creates an environment for novices, foodies and aspiring chefs to learn the tricks of the trade.

Q&A

Karri Schuermans

What tip would you give women
who are starting a business?
Write a succinct business plan, double
the contingency, make sure money
is in the bank before you start, and
have a good support network.

What is your favourite part about
owning a small business?
Flexibility, the ability to react quickly when
opportunities present themselves, being
able to choose who I work with and suppliers
who are a pleasure to do business with.

How do you relax?
Enjoying red wine, dancing,
reading or practicing yoga.

What do you CRAVE?
Fresh cherries, dirt biking, sunsets,
fresh powder, good scotch in good
company and hugs from my kids.

Downtown

CHANGES CLOTHING & JEWELLERY BAR

4454 W 10th Ave, Vancouver, 604.222.1505
changesclothing.com, Twitter: @ChangesGood

Innovative. Trailblazing. Generous.
Changes has rocked the re-sale world since 1997, winning many awards for their outstanding service and leadership. Rhonda Davis drives this thriving clothing and jewellery store with an aim to create a win-win for her customers, staff, community and herself. With a jewellery bar that sparkles with designs by local Canadian artists plus 200 new and like-new high-end fashions daily—*Changes Good!*

Photos by Candice Albach

Rhonda
Davis

⧉ Q&A

What are your most popular
products or services?
A "Diva Den" is a free stylist appointment
at which we can wardrobe clients for an
event or season within any budget. We host
12 events annually and consign daily.

What is your favourite part about
owning a small business?
I love the marketing, management,
leadership and creativity of designing
the excitement that keeps customers
coming back to us, while giving back
generously to my community and world.

What place inspires you and why?
Whitefish, Montana, for its comfort, friendliness
and beauty. Kauai, for its rush of colour
that my eyes can barely keep up with.

Christa
Leigh Meister

Q&A

What is your favourite part about
owning a small business?
Being able to create and watch ideas become
reality without having to be accountable
to anyone but myself and my clients.

Who is your role model or mentor?
My grandfather. He instilled a strong work
ethic in me. His guidance and support made
it possible for me to be where I am today.

What motivates you on a daily basis?
My female clients! Watching a woman
transform herself with just a few simple
wardrobe changes is remarkable, and being
able to play a part in that is very rewarding.

What is your motto or theme song?
"A successful person is one who can lay
a firm foundation with the bricks others
have thrown at him."— David Brinkley

CHRISTA LEIGH
PERSONAL STYLIST AND WARDROBE CONSULTANT

604.315.8887
Twitter: @ChristaLstyle

Renewed. Fresh. Creative.
Christa Leigh, personal stylist and wardrobe consultant, gives women a renewed sense of who they are through coaching, clothing and styling. Whether through an in-home styling session or a personal shopping experience, Christa Leigh assists women in finding comfortable, elegant, stylish clothing, resulting in an effortless, timeless look that embodies all that the female truly is.

Ada Fu and
Miranda Pang

What tip would you give women
who are starting a business?
Take a crash course in Business 101. Learn
the basics of marketing, accounting, business
law, etc. Be original and do something that
speaks to your personality. Don't blindly follow.

What is your favourite part about
owning a small business?
Having our own business is like continually
solving Rubik's cubes. Each problem
is a cube waiting to be solved, and we
celebrate each time we get it right.

What do you CRAVE?
Good white wine, massages, quiet time,
sunny islands, hot bowls of phở and
ramen, sushi and good food in general.

▮ COCOPUNKZ

604.831.7318
cocopunkz.com, Twitter: @cocopunkz

Funky. One-of-a-kind. Unconventional.
Cocopunkz is the collaboration of two women who love shoes
and art. Together, they create one-of-a-kind hand-painted shoes
featuring elaborate illustrations and vivid colours. Each pair of shoes
is lovingly painted and is a unique piece of wearable artwork. If you
have a special occasion to attend or just want something different,
Cocopunkz can work with you to create a customised pair just for you.

COUNTDOWN EVENTS 📞
DESIGN & PLANNING

604.760.8388
countdownevents.com, Twitter: @cremevancouver

Elegant. Awe-inspiring. Distinctive.
CountDown Events produces awe-inspiring events that establish reputations and raise both standards and spirits. Events designed by CountDown Events are inspired by the philosophy of Soha Lavin, founder and creative director of Crème de la Crème Grand Wedding Showcase. Soha and her team of professional planners continue to set the bar for style and elegance with events renowned for their evocative, lavish and exceptional designs.

Soha Lavin

 # Q&A

What are your most popular products or services?
Luxury weddings, innovative corporate events, high society social events, and the Crème de la Crème Grand Wedding Showcase.

What tip would you give women who are starting a business?
Define your goals and objectives, then write a strategic plan and stay the course!

What is your favourite part about owning a small business?
Creative freedom.

What is your motto or theme song?
Everything is possible!

What do you CRAVE?
Riding my Ducati motorcycle.

Stephanie Vogler and Darci Ilich

🏠 Q&A

What are your most popular
products or services?
Custom pillows, upholstery or drapery
(sewn in-house, using elegant fabrics).
Also, our complimentary gift-wrapping and
sought after interior design services.

What is your favourite part about
owning a small business?
The fact that we are able to employ our lovely
staff, and that we provide an escape from
the daily rush to our wonderful clients.

Who is your role model or mentor?
Working moms everywhere.

What place inspires you and why?
The vibrancy of New York City is always
an inspiration. The model off-duty fashion,
the graphic graffiti, textural landscape,
chic restaurants, moody hotel lobbies:
the city never leaves you wanting.

THE CROSS
DECOR AND DESIGN

1198 Homer St, Vancouver, 604.689.2900
thecrossdesign.com, Twitter: @thecrossdesign

Elegant. Classic. Edgy.
In Vancouver's historic Yaletown district and the downtown West End, a 1914 heritage building has been transformed into 5,000 square feet of shopping heaven. The Cross offers a peaceful shopping environment that is complemented with beautifully appointed accessories and found objects, lovely antiques and exquisite furnishings. Since opening in 2003, they have cultivated their brand and developed a loyal and diverse customer base.

Photos by Melissa Gidney Photography

Yaletown

THE DAILEY METHOD

3584 W 41st Ave, Vancouver, 604.266.9191
thedaileymethod.com, Twitter: @TheDaileyMethod, @ TDMVancouver

Effective. Elongating. Strengthening.
The Dailey Method is a unique combination of ballet barre work, core conditioning
and stretching exercises. This challenging one-hour class effectively strengthens,
tones and lengthens the entire body. Light weights are utilized to define the
upper body while mat and ballet work target the thighs, seat and abdominals.
Through this process, your body, alignment and posture will be improved.

Photos by Candice Albach, except main
photo (this page) by Doug McIntosh

Karen Wyder (Owner) and Jey Wyder (Master Instructor)

Q&A

What are your most popular
products or services?
Our class packages and socks with grips.

What tip would you give women
who are starting a business?
Surround yourself with great people.

What motivates you on a daily basis?
Creating something that adds value to the
community and brings more joy to people's lives.

How do you relax?
The Dailey Method! Meditation
and being in nature.

What place inspires you and why?
Being by the ocean or flying puts
everything in perspective.

DELLA OPTIQUE
OPTOMETRY & EYEWEAR

2589 W Broadway, Vancouver, 604.742.3937
dellaoptique.com

Expert. Personal. Delightful.
Remaining at the forefront of the latest eyewear and sunglass trends for more than
10 years, Della Optique's discerning staff provide expert assistance in selection
from an extensive collection of unique designer frames and sunglasses. You
can conveniently have your eyes examined by the eye doctor and get contact
lenses, glasses and sunglasses all in the same location—complete eye care!

Q&A

Dr. Della Chow

What is your favourite part about owning a small business?
The flexibility and freedom to take care of my clients the way I want. Creating a beautiful store and positive environment for my staff and myself. Happy, appreciative clients.

Who is your role model or mentor?
My mentor is my own optometrist who is now retired. I grew up in a small town, Prince George. He treated everyone well and was passionate about his profession.

What is your biggest fear?
My biggest fear is public bathrooms, especially in France.

What place inspires you and why?
The shops and restaurants on my block in Kitsilano. They are mostly small businesses. They are passionate about their products and services, and I get to enjoy the community spirit.

Kitsilano

Shelley Davies

Q&A

What are your most popular products or services?
Kitchen organisation. Originally a place to cook, it has transformed into a multipurpose space to eat meals, do homework, pay bills and use laptops. Organisation is a must.

What tip would you give women who are starting a business?
Start small and dream big. Believe in yourself and don't ever look back. Always remember, mistakes will lead to opportunities.

What place inspires you and why?
Palm Springs for the sunshine, the modern lifestyle and the simple, modern architecture.

What do you CRAVE?
Chocolate, more time with my family, sunshine and success in business!

DETAILS
MODERN ORDER

604.868.2812
detailsmodernorder.com

Transforming. Empowering. Fun.
Residential organising company details MODERN ORDER takes a
modern approach to an organised life: live with only those things you love,
use, wear and cherish. Shelley Davies works side by side with clients to
create personalised spaces that are clutter-free, organised, simplified
and beautiful. The "less is more" mantra of details MODERN ORDER
is what creates homes that are spacious, calm and stress-free.

Caree Bray

Q&A

What are your most popular products or services?
It's really dependent on finding the right fit for each individual's needs, be it a new home purchase, debt consolidation, refinance or home equity line of credit.

What is your favourite part about owning a small business?
The flexibility allows me to meet my clients on their terms, when and where it's convenient for them.

Who is your role model or mentor?
My amazing group of girlfriends who all inspire me with their unique strengths and aspirations.

How do you relax?
I turn off my BlackBerry and open a book or indulge in my secret obsession, reality TV.

☎ DOMINION LENDING CENTRES LEADING EDGE

201-15955 Fraser Hwy, Surrey, 604.836.4613
careebray.ca, Twitter: @careebray

Convenient. Trustworthy. Dynamic.
Caree Bray is a licensed mortgage professional and partner of Kaerus
Group, powered by Dominion Lending Centres. With a passion for
real estate finance, Caree builds and maintains long-term financial
relationships with her clients. She makes shopping for a mortgage
stress-free and provides peace of mind; as a client, you'll know that you
received the best product available. Best of all, her services are *free*!

ISHARA photographed by Melissa Gidney Photography

What is your motto or theme song?

 If you want to achieve greatness, stop asking for permission.

Amrit Baidwan of ISHARA

DREAM DESIGNS

956 Commercial Dr, Vancouver, 604.254.5012
1277 Lynn Valley Rd, North Vancouver, 604.929.3318
1502 Marine Dr, West Vancouver, 604.922.8325
dreamdesigns.ca

Stylish. Organic. Sustainable.
The atmosphere at Dream Designs is naturally calming and inspiring.
Founded in 1981, Dream Designs is a premier destination for stylish
organic linens and mattresses, clothing and accessories for yoga and
meditations, decor and more. Many of their products are made locally in
Dream Designs' own workshop, complemented by a wide array of well-made
sustainable products sourced both locally and responsibly worldwide.

Photos by Jordana Dhahan of Through the Looking Glass Photography

Linda Tang

 # Q&A

What are your most popular
products or services?
Organic cotton bed linens and mattresses;
kapok, wool and buckwheat pillows;
bamboo, silk and wool duvets; organic
cotton towels; and Hemp shower curtains.

What tip would you give women
who are starting a business?
Believe in your dreams and learn from your
failures—you'll have many, but it's okay.
Also, pay close attention to your cash flow.

What place inspires you and why?
The planet we live on because it gives us
life and provides everything we need.

What do you CRAVE?
World peace and to achieve meaningful
connections with others through my work.

Sarah Shore and
Geneve McNally

 Q&A

What is your favourite part about
owning a small business?
We love that we are responsible for our
own success. It's up to us to make room
for our next big idea! We love inspiring
greatness in ourselves and others.

Who is your role model or mentor?
Fellow industry leaders who are making
waves, past employers who offered
encouragement toward success, our
families without whom we could not do
what we do. Martha Stewart and Oprah.

What motivates you on a daily basis?
As business partners and friends for 13 years,
we are polar opposites bringing different
strengths to the table. Constantly challenging
one another keeps us sharp and on our toes!

☎ DREAMGROUP PRODUCTIONS
WEDDING & EVENT PLANNERS

604.537.3575
dreamgroup.ca, Twitter: @DreamGroup

Vibrant. Inspiring. Dedicated.
DreamGroup Productions lives, breathes and loves weddings. Their clients are busy couples looking to create an unforgettable and efficiently executed wedding affair. DreamGroup planners understand how to move a client through a successful planning experience, taking into consideration the client's vision, style and budget expectations. They have built their reputation on being experts in their field, showing great passion and confidence in everything they do.

Main photo (this page) and top left and middle photos (opposite page) by Studio-O portrait by Jonetsu Photography, top right photo (opposite page) by Josh Bowie

DUTCH GIRL CHOCOLATES

1002 Commercial Drive, Vancouver, 604.251.3221

Sweet. Luscious. Tempting.
It's electrifying to walk into this chocolate and candy haven of walls, counters and jars of all things yummy. Handmade Belgian chocolates are made right before your eyes. Dutch and German sweet and salty licorices, imported candies and nostalgic treats may make your head spin in this nod to an old-fashioned sort of emporium.

Alexandra Temple

Q&A

What are your most popular
products or services?
Handmade chocolates with pure, fresh
ingredients, and absolutely no preservatives.
More than 70 different kinds of imported
licorices and exotic and old-fashioned candies.

What is your biggest fear?
When I first opened, my biggest fear was
that I would not enjoy dealing with the
public. Now, one of my favourite things
is chatting with our lovely customers.

What place inspires you and why?
The Pemberton Valley—it shows me
every time how incredibly fortunate we
are to live in such a beautiful province.

What do you CRAVE?
Where to start? Going out of town, music,
good friends, yummy food, a nice glass of
wine, preferably all at the same time!

Jessica Hill

Q&A

What are your most popular products or services?
Women love ecocessories' Everyday Earrings, which are perfect for the active lifestyles of moms, athletes, travelers and busy professionals!

What tip would you give women who are starting a business?
Believe in yourself, express confidence and let passion drive you every day.

What is your motto or theme song?
Live with passion.

What do you CRAVE?
A world where people naturally make choices in consideration of the environment and accept responsibility for making this world a better place!

Photos by Brian Hill Photography, except portrait

ECOCESSORIES

ecocessories.ca, Twitter: @ecocessories

Stylish. Timeless. Unique.
Ecocessories is an eco-friendly jewellery design company featuring
jewelry hand-crafted from precious metals and recycled beads. For
women with old, broken, unwanted jewelry, ecocessories offers a jewelry
recycling service—drop off your pieces at two Vancouver locations
or recycle online. Driven by a passion for sustainability and fashion,
shop for new eco-jewelry designs at boutiques across Canada!

ELEMENTS MINERAL MAKEUP

elementsminerals.com, Twitter: @elementsmakeup

Current. Healthy. Sexy.
Elements Mineral Makeup was created from a passion for health, wellness and beauty. They offer solutions to the sophisticated women of today who are seeking makeup products free of parabens, fillers, preservatives, chemicals and dyes. The high quality of Elements Mineral Makeup provides customers with only pure crushed minerals and simple clean beauty.

Q&A

What are your most popular products or services?
Our most popular eye shadows are Tuxedo White, Oyster, Brix and Espresso. Our foundations have become a hit because they are light, offer great coverage and are perfect for humid weather.

Who is your role model or mentor?
We love Chip Wilson, founder of Lululemon! He is a brilliant businessman and visionary.

What motivates you on a daily basis?
We are inspired by positive feedback from the women wearing our products and seeing their confidence and delight from wearing healthy and high-quality makeup.

What do you CRAVE?
Educating women about what is in their makeup, knowing their options, and learning how to read the ingredient labels.

Kelli Taylor
and Ozzie Kipnes

I am natural beauty

elements
MINERAL MAKEUP

Kelli Taylor

Q&A

What is your favourite part about owning a small business?
I love the freedom to make final decisions and bringing people together to create a strong team and a successful business.

What motivates you on a daily basis?
Knowing that I am making a difference in people's lives just by helping them heal their bodies and get their health back.

What is your motto or theme song?
Success is not the key to happiness. Happiness is the key to success. If you love what you are doing, you will be successful.

How do you relax?
I relax by walking the beach every night with my family and enjoying the spectacular view of the mountains and the city.

ELEMENTS WELLNESS CENTRE

2678 W Broadway, Ste 207, Vancouver, 604.732.9355
elementswellnesscentre.com, Twitter: @elementscentre

Healing. Revitalizing. Tranquil.
Elements Wellness is a multidisciplinary centre in Kitsilano. They offer the very best in both therapeutic and spa services. Their expertise, knowledge and diverse therapies allow people many avenues to choose from when looking to heal their body or for a preventative plan for health and wellness. A safe, relaxing and comfortable environment is made for each of their guests.

Photos by Sukhi Ghuman Photography

Kitsilano

ELSA CORSI

692 Seymour St, Vancouver, 604.687.5577
elsacorsi.com, Twitter: @elsa_corsi

Beautiful. Custom. Timeless.
Inspired by the grandeur of Old Hollywood and red carpet sensibility, jewellery that carries the mark of ELSA CORSI are endearing and important symbols that define the new generation of couture costume jewellery. Using second-generation techniques passed on from a master stone setter and crystal enthusiast, ELSA CORSI jewellery is a favourite among Vancouver stylists, costume designers and socialites seeking a dramatic, sparkly touch.

Elsa Corsi

Q&A

What are your most popular products or services?
I am famous for my dramatic chandelier earrings. It's even been reported that Gwen Stefani once drooled over a pair during an interview with a local reporter.

What is your favourite part about owning a small business?
I am thankful that I am not at a job where I have to count the days until the weekend. Every day can be whatever I choose to make of it.

What place inspires you and why?
The jewellery department at Bergdorf Goodman in New York. Their selection of designers is spectacular and to one day be in their company is definitely in the five-year plan.

What do you CRAVE?
Japanese Nail Art Manicures by Yasushi and the Decked Out Caesar at Coast.

Stefania
Polopoli

 Q&A

What are your most popular
products or services?
We offer everything from hair, skin and nail
services to tanning. Excentric has it all.

What tip would you give women
who are starting a business?
Believe in your dream. I was always told that
I should take the "safe" route and because
I didn't, I have a successful salon!

What is your favourite part about
owning a small business?
The feeling of accomplishment and freedom.

Who is your role model or mentor?
My parents.

What is your biggest fear?
I don't fear anything. I take what comes
my way and always learn from it.

Burnaby

EXCENTRIC SALON

4525 Hastings St, Burnaby, 604.298.1838
excentricsalon.com, Twitter: @ExcentricSalon

Stylish. Flirty. Chic.
Trendy decor, great products and amazing staff fill Excentric Salon. Whether you're looking for relaxing pedicures, tanning services or the perfect hairstyle, you're sure to find it here. Experience the warm, comforting atmosphere at Excentric while discovering the beauty goddess in you!

FAVOURITE GIFTS

Lonsdale Quay Market (2nd Level): 204-123 Carrie Cates Court, North Vancouver
604.904.8840
favouritegifts.ca, Twitter: @favouritegifts

Fresh. Fabulous. Local.
Favourite Gifts, located in the Lonsdale Quay Market, is a go-to spot
to find that perfect gift or a special little treat for yourself. Each item is
carefully handpicked by owner Carol Hyslop, bringing together the finest
in locally made jewellery, handbags, stationery, baby gifts and more!

Photos by Sukhi Ghuman Photography

Carol Hyslop

Q&A

What tip would you give women
who are starting a business?
Know your limitations and when to delegate.
Focus your energy where your strengths
are, which are probably the most important
aspects of your business anyway.

What is your favourite part about
owning a small business?
Everything! I get to surround myself with
beautiful objects, created by people who I
know, like and respect, and then share them
with the loveliest customers in the world!

How do you relax?
Running on the trails or the seawall,
meeting friends for coffee or a pint
or curling up with a good book.

North Vancouver

FEEL FABULOUS MOBILE SPA

123-1208 Homer St, Vancouver, 604.568.6800
feelfabulous.ca

Girly. Creative. Educational.
For a day, girls get to be girls, enjoying some of the things girls enjoy most!
Feel Fabulous Mobile Spa has several birthday party packages that include a
combination of mini-manicures and pedicures with nail art, facials, hairstyling, light
makeup applications, and activities where the girls can make their own beauty
products. You can bring the girls into the spa or the spa can come to you!

Catherine Lalonde

Q&A

What are your most popular
products or services?
Our facial, manicure and pedicure package.
Girls learn skincare basics, how to make a
homemade facial mask from several natural and
organic ingredients, and also get pretty nails!

What tip would you give women
who are starting a business?
Learn to sacrifice and be patient, pour your
heart into your work, keep a positive attitude
and energy, live with passion and purpose,
challenge your fears and follow your dreams.

What is your favourite part about
owning a small business?
Having creative freedom. I love being able to
envision ideas, put ideas into action, and see
my dreams and passions come to fruition.

What do you CRAVE?
Banana ice cream and banana smoothies!

Yaletown

Fiona Louie

Q&A

What are your most popular products or services?
Necklaces are popular in a variety of designs. Everyone has their story on how the piece is special to them and symbolizes a part of their life.

What tip would you give women who are starting a business?
Be prepared for a lot of hard work and don't lose sight of your vision.

What is your favourite part about owning a small business?
I find it very rewarding to see my business grow and my dream become reality.

How do you relax?
Travel, sunshine and beaches!

FILOU DESIGNS

604.728.0239
filoudesigns.com, Twitter: @filoudesigns

Canadian. Handcrafted. Unique.
Filou Designs features original nature-inspired sterling silver and 24-karat gold vermeil jewellery designs created by artist Fiona Louie in signature cutout silhouette, medallion and 3-D styles. Find that special piece for everyday wear, to layer on dressy occasions or for a treasured gift. You can find Filou at fine boutiques and galleries across Canada. Adorn yourself with jewels that mean something. Which piece speaks to you?

FINE FINDS

1014 Mainland St, Vancouver, 604.669.8325
finefindsboutique.com, Twitter: @finefinds

Interesting. Reliable. Fun.
Fine Finds is the perfect one-stop shop to find the complete outfit and the perfect gift. The complete outfit includes shoes, handbag, jewels, polish, headpiece and, of course, the apparel that asks the question, "Where did you get your dress? I love it!" Fine Finds has been a Yaletown fixture for more than 10 years and we know why!

Jane McFadden
and Megan Maxwell

 Q&A

What are your most popular
products or services?
Clothing, jewelry, handbags and a
huge selection of gifts for you, the
kids and your favourite aunt.

What tip would you give women
who are starting a business?
You must commit yourself 100 percent to the
business and make that your priority. It will
always be more demanding than you think.

What is your favourite part about
owning a small business?
Working with one another, making our own
decisions and providing a nice place to work.

What is your biggest fear?
Getting old too fast.

Yaletown

Gloria
Cheung

 # Q&A

What are your most popular
products or services?
Custom hand-tied floral bouquets and
arrangements. We also are known for our
excellent work at weddings and events.

What tip would you give women
who are starting a business?
Really love what you do. Have
a passion for your work.

What motivates you on a daily basis?
Personally striving for creative excellence in
design, providing work that is enjoyed and
loved by the people who use our services,
and being a leader in my community.

How do you relax?
Playing with my young son or watching
really cheesy Jane Austen movies.

✳ THE FLOWER FACTORY

3604 Main St, 604.871.1008
flowerfactory.ca

Innovative. Stylish. Fresh.
The Flower Factory has become a leading flower boutique in
Vancouver. Providing fresh, creative floral designs that meet
individual needs, The Flower Factory serves the greater Vancouver
area while still retaining a neighbourhood-store feel.

Photos by Candice Albach, except portrait by Angela Hubbard Photography

Main Street

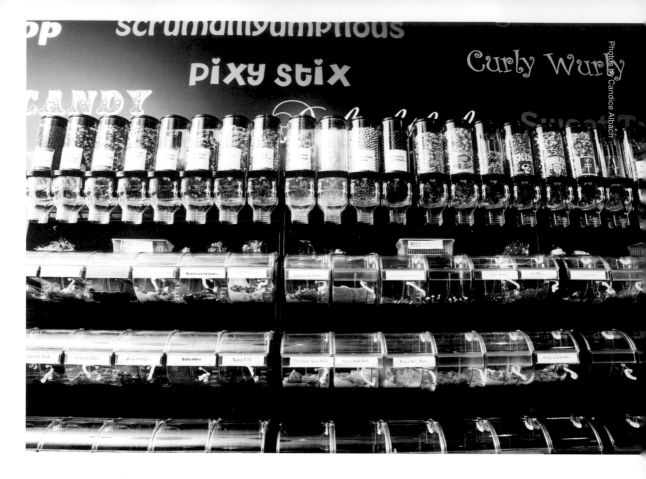

FRANKIES CANDY BAR

5305 West Blvd, Vancouver, 604.568.3107
2451 Marine Dr, West Vancouver, 604.922.8291
frankiescandybar.com, Twitter: @sweetfrankies

Scrumdidlyumptious. Whimsical. Delightful.
Frankies Candy Bar is a boutique candy store offering sweet treats from around the world. Family-owned and -operated by the Caruk sisters, Frankies is a candy wonderland for the young and young at heart. The sisters love to travel in search of unique and delicious confectionery delights that bring joy to their customers. Creativity and passion make Frankies Candy Bar a delectable destination.

Jennifer and Lisa Caruk

Q&A

What are your most popular products or services?
Frankies goody bags, gift baskets and candy buffets are always a hit. Our top three sweet treats are chocolate-covered gummy bears, silver cola balls and sour rainbow belts.

What motivates you on a daily basis?
When customers leave with smiles on their faces and a bag full of candy, you know they had an experience they will remember.

What is your motto or theme song?
Life is *sweet*.

What do you CRAVE?
Jennifer: An afternoon nap and candy!
Lisa: Spending time with my gorgeous niece, Peyton. We both have an obsession with bubble tea.

Eliza Lau

Q&A

Who is your role model or mentor?
Anyone who has started their own successful business. I had no idea it would be as difficult as it is!

What motivates you on a daily basis?
I used to dress models and actors. Now I dress ordinary people and find it so much more gratifying. I'm motivated by how happy people are when they leave my shop.

What is your favourite part about owning a small business?
I have control over what happens (mostly anyway).

What is your motto or theme song?
Don't do it unless it's fun.

GENTILLE ALOUETTE

227 Carrall St, Vancouver, 604.688.6819
gentille-alouette.com, Twitter: @eliza_lau

Whimsical. Eclectic. Playful.
Eliza is a fashion stylist and special effects costumer for the film industry. Her latest love affair with fashion and textiles has come in the form of her newly opened boutique, Gentille Alouette. Gentille Alouette is a visionary response by Eliza to bridge fashion and art. Consciously created to push the limit of creativity, Gentille Alouette houses some of the best talent in Canada.

GINA BEST

1-155 Water St, Vancouver, 604.730.5020
meridianpacific.ca, Twitter: @meridianpacific

Professional. Personable. Resourceful.
Gina Best, owner of Mortgage Alliance Meridian Pacific, has been voted
one of the best mortgage brokers in Vancouver. She takes the time to
get to know her clients and help them by providing the right mortgage
for their lifestyle. Gina not only will get you the "best" mortgage for
you but will manage your mortgage for as long as you have it.

▪Q&A

Gina Best

What tip would you give women
who are starting a business?
Get your message clear and go out
and network, network, network.

What is your favourite part about
owning a small business?
Freedom. I can make my own hours and I
am in charge. I get to come up with ideas
and I get to make them come to life.

What motivates you on a daily basis?
Helping others. That is what I am all about, for
me that is what is behind almost everything I do.

What is your motto or theme song?
From *Finding Nemo*: "Just keep
swimming, swimming, swimming."

What place inspires you and why?
Places with lots of people. I wonder what
their stories are. That sets my imagination
going and give me the best ideas.

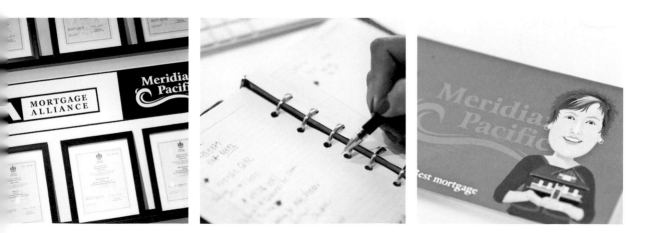

Andrea Warner

◧ Q&A

What are your most popular
products or services?
Wedding photography and lifestyle portraits.

What tip would you give women
who are starting a business?
Perseverance is one of the most important
qualities you can maintain. Set out on the
course to reach your dream, make mistakes,
make changes and keep on going.

What is your motto or theme song?
Joseph Campbell's famous
quote, "Follow your bliss."

What do you CRAVE?
Laughing so hard that it makes me cry,
the first snow of winter, my husband's
sweet smile and, of course, chocolate.

☎ GO-LUCKY PHOTOGRAPHY

778.245.3686
goluckyphoto.com, Twitter: @GoLuckyPhoto

Modern. Expressive. Spontaneous.
Go-Lucky Photography was started by Andrea Warner, a graduate of the
Emily Carr University and internationally published wedding and portrait
photographer. Andrea's photographic approach is spontaneous and relaxed,
while anticipating those moments that you wish to remember forever.
With a modern, photojournalistic style, Go-Lucky Photography captures
the moments that make your day truly unique and unforgettable.

Photos by Go-Lucky Photography

⬛ Q&A

What are your most popular products or services?
The Truffle Pig Chocolate Bars and Truffle Piglets.

What tip would you give women who are starting a business?
Success comes to those who hang on when all others have given up!

What is your favourite part about owning a small business?
I like the versatility, flexibility and freedom. Plus, I get to eat as much chocolate as I want every day!

Who is your role model or mentor?
At different points in my life and for various reasons I have had different role models but for the overall woman, Audrey Hepburn.

Shelley Wallace

HAGENSBORG CHOCOLATES

604.215.0234
hagensborg.com, Twitter: @trufflepigbar

High-quality. Playful. Genuine.
In the chocolate kingdom located in Burnaby BC, the reigning princess, assisted by her team of princesses-in-waiting, produces and markets some of the finest European chocolates in all the land. Featuring Snuffly the Truffle Pig, these treats are master-crafted using all-natural European ingredients and can be found throughout Canada, the United States, England and Japan.

Holly Wong

Q&A

What are your most popular products or services?
Jewellery by House of Harlow, Low Luv by Erin Wasson, and accessories by C.Pak & Co. However, what really makes Holly shine are the many dresses that range from casual to dressy.

What motivates you on a daily basis?
What really motivates me is when customers appreciate what we are doing with the store and fall in love with the lines we carry.

What place inspires you and why?
The big fashion cities inspire me because I enjoy observing people's everyday wear. I love seeing other people's point of view through their attire and how they accessorize to represent themselves.

What do you CRAVE?
Sunshine, Big City red velvet cupcakes and fun customers!

HOLLY

215-332 Water St (2nd entrance at Cordova and Homer), Vancouver, 604.681.8883
shopholly.ca, Twitter: @hollyboutique

Flirty. Feminine. Fabulous.
Located in the heart of Gastown, Holly brings new flavor to the area.
The basis of the boutique is to provide fun, trendy, feminine pieces that
easily transition from work to play. Bringing new labels to the city with a
glam-girl-meets-rocker-chick feel. You will surely find a strong mixture
of styles and labels that aren't as easily accessible in the city.

Photos by Melissa Gidney Photography

KV BIJOU photographed by Bopomo Pictures

What tip would you give women who are starting a business?

"Love what you do. Do it honestly, invest all your passion and don't expect anything in return. Success will come in its own way— it can't be forced."

Maureen Welton of 18KARAT

I LOVE MY MUFF

ilovemymuff.com, Twitter: @ilovemymuff

Bold. Fresh. Sassy.
I Love My Muff is an eco-chic line of premium feminine-care products.
Handmade in Canada with love, their products promise to provide
daily love and care for down there. This bold brand launched in NYC
at high end retailer Henri Bendel in 2009 and has since expanded
into many major cities across North America and Europe.

Photos by Melissa Gidney Photography

Ritz Clinging

 Q&A

What are your most popular products or services?
Our muff maintenance kits are the best sellers. They offer all four of our products in a great package that's ideal for travel, and they make fantastic gifts too.

Who is your role model or mentor?
My mom and my sisters. I'm blessed to have such strong women in my life. My husband; he's incredibly driven. I'm inspired by his tenacity.

What is your biggest fear?
Being afraid to fail. If you're afraid to fail you'll never try anything.

What is your motto or theme song?
"Empire State of Mind." We launched in New York, so it has a personal connection for me. "Concrete jungles where dreams are made of, there's nothing you can't do."

IMPULSE SPORT THERAPEUTICS

205-130 Brew St, Port Moody, 604.949.1515
impulsesport.ca

Innovative. Healthy. Friendly.
Impulse is Port Moody's most comprehensive multidisciplinary rehabilitation clinic. With an integrated team of specialised professionals, they provide some of the best health care in Vancouver. The team at Impulse also keeps in mind the wellbeing of the environment and global community with a paperless system, green products and a portion of treatment fees going to support international health projects—so clients can help others by helping themselves!

 # Q&A

Leah Davis

What tip would you give women
who are starting a business?
Perfection from the start is impossible, so give
yourself the freedom to change and grow.
Evolve and learn from achievements and
failures—they're both progress, so take risks!

What motivates you on a daily basis?
I love to make a difference for others and
I am motivated by seeing any positive
change that is possible in health, quality
of life, knowledge or business.

What is your motto or theme song?
"You Learn" by Alanis Morissette
always reminds me that I can grow
and learn from every experience.

What do you CRAVE?
I crave laughter, color, balance, campfires,
learning, fresh air, holding hands,
bare feet in sand, mangos, live music,
time with friends and adventure.

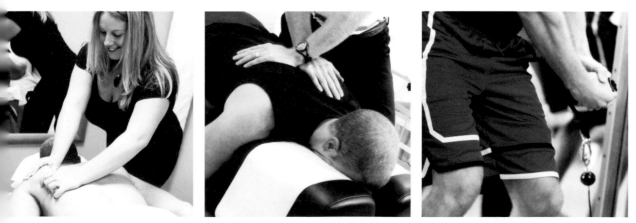

Margaret Dron

Q&A

What are your most popular products or services?
Mortgage plans. Low rates are just the beginning. Utilizing my education and background in finance and strategic planning, I will create a mortgage plan that's right for your life.

What tip would you give women who are starting a business?
Keep a journal of your goals and successes (yes, even the little ones) to keep you focused and inspired during challenging days.

Who is your role model or mentor?
Rob King and Laurie Schultz. They taught and inspired me to look beyond just the numbers to truly succeed in business. It's about people.

What is your biggest fear?
Losing my BlackBerry.

Margaret Dron
Mortgage Broker

invis
Canada's Mortgage Experts

Phone 604.430.2090
Fax 604.998.2243
Cell 778.888.6274
www.BCMortgageAdvice.com
mdron@BCMortgageAdvice.com

INVIS

604.430.2090
bcmortgageadvice.com, Twitter: @MargaretDron

Personable. Analytical. Compassionate.
As an Invis mortgage broker, Margaret Dron provides expert, unbiased advice to home buyers or those looking to renew or refinance their mortgage, lease business equipment or consolidate debts. By not being tied to just one specific bank, Margaret uses her relationships with more than 60 national and regional lenders to evaluate and plan the best mortgage for you.

INVITO COUTURE

1189-88 W Pender St, Vancouver, 604.681.3464
invitocouture.com, Twitter: @invitocouture

European. Elegant. Stylish.
Invito Couture is a downtown boutique offering high-quality European evening gowns, cocktail dresses, and prom and bridesmaid dresses, along with a selection of fashion jewellery and accessories. All dresses are made in Turkey using Turkish and Italian fabrics in more than 100 different styles. Limited quantities of each dress are kept in-store to retain exclusivity, although custom sizes and orders are available.

Liz Delaney

 # Q&A

What are your most popular products or services?
Cocktail dresses are the most popular item since they can be worn to both casual and formal events. Our customers also love that we offer free alterations on all evening gowns.

Who is your role model or mentor?
My parents who have owned their own business for more than 30 years.

What motivates you on a daily basis?
The success of my business. I like seeing what will happen next each day and being able to successfully overcome the obstacles.

What place inspires you and why?
Turkey inspires me because of its sophisticated citizens and high level of European fashion.

IS. SALON

1260 Hamilton St, Vancouver, 604.569.HAIR (604.569.4247)
issalon.ca, Twitter: @issalon

Modern. Comfortable. Fun.
Is. Salon is home to some of Vancouver's top stylists and makeup artists.
Stylists have been trained internationally in cities such as London, Los
Angeles and New York. A comfortable and friendly atmosphere combined
with talented individuals creates the perfect environment for creativity
to blossom. Is. Salon is not only one of the best places in the city for a
cut and colour, but also for extensions and the Brazilian Blowdry.

Erin Moore

Q&A

What are your most popular
products or services?
The Brazilian Blowdry or Keratin Smoothing
System. It is an amazing treatment that
reconstructs hair and eliminates frizz.
We also specialise in extensions.

What is your favourite part about
owning a small business?
The freedom to create your environment.
Owning my own business has allowed me the
freedom to create a pleasurable place for clients,
staff and myself to return to again and again.

What do you CRAVE?
I crave knowledge. I love to learn. I can't
wait to learn about new services and
products in the beauty industry, and am
always the first to try new things.

Yaletown

ISHARA

38 Water St, Vancouver, 604.264.7494
shopishara.com, Twitter: @shopishara

Feminine. Bold. Exclusive.
ISHARA is a tightly edited assortment of exceptional collections inspired by
luxury. ISHARA ("to send someone in the right direction"), is an exclusive
boutique where people can peek through carefully selected racks of
contemporary designer garments, accessories and jewellery. Frequented
by both fashionistas and stylish professionals, the sophisticated boutique is
renowned for its hip and friendly atmosphere and buzz-worthy events.

Amrit
Baidwan

▥ Q&A

What are your most popular
products or services?
Popular collections include Smythe blazers,
White + Warren cashmere, Akiko dresses and
Rich & Skinny denim. Customers also love
booking personal shopping appointments
and private shopping parties for a more
personal and unique experience.

What is your favourite part about
owning a small business?
I love having a creative outlet where
I can use all of my past experience,
education and interests to create
something I—and our customers—love.

What is your motto or theme song?
If you want to achieve greatness,
stop asking for permission.

What do you CRAVE?
A sense of calm and satisfaction—
both in business and life!

Q&A

What are your most popular
products or services?
Our 75-litre moving crates, which
are manufactured in Canada with 95
percent recycled plastic and have a
life expectancy of 10–12 years. Some
of them are on their 500th move.

What tip would you give women
who are starting a business?
Listen without judgement, seek knowledge and
strive to become the authority in your field.

What place inspires you and why?
Beautiful BC and the people who call it
home. West coasters are progressive,
love their environment and work
collectively to keep it pristine. There's no
better place to be an eco-preneur.

Carrie
Dhensaw

IT'S YOUR MOVE

604.835.7225
saynotoboxes.com, Twitter: @saynotoboxes

Genuine. Smart. Flexible.
Countering the myth that eco-friendly products and services come
at a cost disincentive, It's Your Move encourages consumers to "think
outside the cardboard box" by promoting a convenient, cost-effective and
eco-friendly alternative to the use of wasteful cardboard boxes for moving.
It's Your Move provides a rental service of heavy-duty reusable moving
crates and supplies throughout the Lower Mainland and Fraser Valley.

Main photo (this page) and portrait by Dana Dykman, top left photos
(opposite page) by Todd Duncalski of Todd's Photos

Julia Linford

 Q&A

What are your most popular
products or services?
The Original Organic Facial and Himalayan Salt
Detox Scrub in combination with an Infrared
Sauna. J Naturals is J spa's exclusive skin care
line—100 percent pure from plant oils and fruits.

Who is your role model or mentor?
My father. He is a very successful
businessman who makes his own products
and sells them across the country. Truly
inspiring, he is a huge support to me.

What motivates you on a daily basis?
Waking up every day with a fresh new
start... creative ideas, health and wellness,
women in business and culture!

Photos by Jordana Dhahan of Through the Looking Glass Photography

J SPA

276 E 2nd Ave, Vancouver, 778.229.1510
j-spa.ca

Luxurious. Pampering. Exclusive.
J spa is a modern boutique spa, offering high-end, organic treatments
and products such as Eminence Organics and J Naturals, J spa's
exclusive face/body care line. Specialising in facials and decadent body
treatments, we love to pamper you in our intimate, luxurious setting,
providing an experience that has you coming back for more.

JAG DHAHAN
MAKEUP ARTIST &
CLINICAL ESTHETICIAN

778.772.3301
jagdhahan.com

Flawless. Beautiful. Healthy.
As well as being a professionally certified makeup artist, Jag Dhahan is also
a clinical esthetician and laser technician and currently manages an anti-
aging laser clinic. Her ongoing training, dedication and experience along
with her friendly personality provide clients with an artistically versatile
experience. Jag enjoys working with different ethnicities and complexions.
She is also committed to providing her clients with only the best products. Jag
now offers St. Tropez sunless spray tanning and Smile FX teeth whitening.

Jag Dhahan

Q&A

What are your most popular products or services?
Makeup applications and enzyme facial peels.

What tip would you give women who are starting a business?
Stay organized.

What is your favourite part about owning a small business?
Being in charge of my schedule.

How do you relax?
Cuddling with my dog on the couch.

What place inspires you and why?
The ocean because of its energy.

What do you CRAVE?
Vacations.

JERICHO COUNSELLING

400-601 W Broadway, Vancouver
300-1055 W Hastings St, Vancouver
206-5050 Kingsway, Burnaby
604.434.5727
jerichocounselling.com

Accessible. Affordable. Confidential.
Jericho Counselling is a great choice for urban women and men in the Lower
Mainland looking for counselling. Their offices are beautifully decorated
in terrific locations and their therapists offer the kind of counselling and
support we have all been looking for: therapists who you can relate to, who
work evenings and weekends and who will reply to your text messages.

Dawn Schooler, M.A., R.C.C.

 # Q&A

What is your favourite part about owning a small business?
The freedom to do what I love and to help as many people as I can.

What is your motto or theme song?
"Where Is the Love" by the Black Eyed Peas. Modern counselling is about helping people find "the love" and is a political act. Helping one helps hundreds.

What place inspires you and why?
That quiet place deep inside my heart (and yours) where I know that everything is okay. I am okay. The world is going to be okay.

What do you CRAVE?
I crave a world where counselling is embraced by and encouraged for anyone who simply wants to feel better.

Joanna Konkin

Q&A

What are your most popular products or services?
Our most popular service is nail art—sometimes even at a party in a client's home. Our most popular product is the Bota-peptide Eye Cream, which has five different actions!

What is your favourite part about owning a small business?
I am a free spirit and an independent person, so I like having my own schedule and being flexible. My business has also really helped me grow as a person.

What is your motto or theme song?
"All that we are is the result of what we have thought. The mind is everything, what you think, you become."—Buddha

Photos by Tracey Ayton Photography

South Granville

JO'S TOES & ESTHETICS

212-2233 Burrard St, Vancouver, 604.736.1200
jostoes.com

Bright. Serene. Creative.
Jo's Toes & Esthetics has been helping both women and men look
and feel their best since 2002. Jo's Toes is known for custom, hand-
painted nail art with hundreds of colours and patterns to choose from.
Jo's Toes also provides full esthetic services and is conveniently located
in the heart of Kits, with a relaxing garden view of a lush courtyard.

Julie
Tidiman

Q&A

What are your most popular
products or services?
Personalised real estate representation—
buying, selling, new construction. I also support
paperless transactions, reusable moving crates,
energy assessments and avoid junk mail.

What is your favourite part about
owning a small business?
The freedom to create and execute my own
personal vision of my business and ideal life.

What is your motto or theme song?
"Well-behaved women rarely make
history!"—Laurel Thatcher Ulrich

What do you CRAVE?
A killer life, honest love, happy family,
cozy home, successful career, financial
freedom, sunshine, powder days, good
surf and an abundance of wine.

JULIE TIDIMAN, REALTOR®

604.626.6066
thinkjulie.com, Twitter: @thinkjulie

Smart. Personal. Fun.
As a real estate agent with Sutton 1st West Realty, Julie Tidiman provides smart and honest real estate representation while getting to know her clients and their desires. Armed with this information, her skills, knowledge, personality and a plan, Julie personalises the entire real estate experience. Creative marketing, constant communication and smart negotiations are standard. Julie's relaxed approach takes the stress out of the most difficult situations and makes her clients feel safe, informed and confident.

Photos by Bopomo Pictures

Jennifer Hood

Q&A

What are your most popular
products or services?
Although our weekly classes and birthday
parties are the most popular, our Date Nights
create the most buzz in the community—what
parent isn't looking for an adult night out?

What tip would you give women
who are starting a business?
Surround yourself with the best team possible;
let the professionals do what they do best
and free up your time to focus on growth.

What is your biggest fear?
Running out of time before I have a
chance to tackle all of my ideas.

How do you relax?
Summer evening meals in the garden
with friends and family, and long winter
hikes through the misty woods.

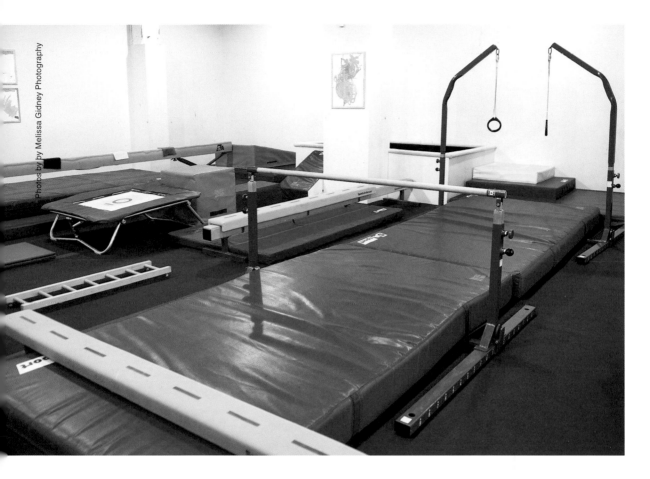

▚ JUMP! GYMNASTICS

101-837 Beatty St, Vancouver, 604.568.9690
jumpgymnastics.ca, Twitter: @jumpgym

Playful. Welcoming. Innovative.
Jump! Gymnastics offers a unique physical activity program for children from six months to eight years old in their child-inspired facility. They focus on physical literacy, giving children the tools they need to become active for life, regardless of what sports interest them as they grow. Since they provide programs to more than 500 kids a week at their flagship facility, growth plans are in the near future!

Yaletown

Photos by Bopomo Pictures

KV BIJOU

kvbijou.com, Twitter: @kvbijou

Vibrant. Unique. Chic.
KV BIJOU is handcrafted, nature-inspired sterling silver jewellery by designer
Kelsey Vanderhorst. This young, trendsetting company has been seen in *Flare*,
Allure, *US Weekly*, and *The New York Times*. With a growing celebrity clientele,
KV BIJOU was worn by Ali Fedotowsky on season 14 of *The Bachelorette*.
Known for its keen design sense, this is a company to keep an eye on!

Kelsey
Vanderhorst

 # Q&A

What are your most popular
products or services?
Often, after a client purchases KV BIJOU, they
can't stop! Many pieces are limited edition
and my loyal clients are always excited for
new designs to add to their collections.

What tip would you give women
who are starting a business?
Be prepared to work like never before!

What is your favourite part about
owning a small business?
Being my own boss and having the chance
to do my dream job as my career. I love the
creative freedom and limitless possibilities.

How do you relax?
Laughing with my husband, taking on a
new creative project, taking a hot bath,
going shopping, playing my piano, prayer
and by seeing friends or family.

LAKSHMI

2868 W Broadway, Vancouver, 604.568.3883
lakshmiboutique.com

Feminine. Glamourous. Exclusive.
LAKSHMI is a go-to boutique for something pretty and stylish. Situated in Kitsilano,
LAKSHMI is an ultra-chic haunt you'd find on Melrose Avenue, where you can
confidently shop without breaking the bank. Sisters Preetka and Sarah Brar travel
the globe to source out stylish lines of clothing and accessories, so that you will
not be caught wearing the same outfit as every other Vancouver fashionista.

Photos by Jordana Dhahan of Through the Looking Glass Photography

Sarah and Preetka Brar

 Q&A

What are your most popular
products or services?
Our dresses. In particular, the Goddess
Dress, designed in-house, has been
our best-selling dress for the past three
years. Made of 100 percent silk, it drapes
beautifully on every body type.

What tip would you give women
who are starting a business?
We started with a dream, we believed
in the dream and, in turn, we are living
our dream. Visualize what you want to
achieve and always dream *big*.

What is your motto or theme song?
"Dress Like a Goddess." LAKSHMI boutique is
inspired by the Indian goddess, Lakshmi. As the
goddess of wealth and beauty, she's personified
as the embodiment of loveliness and grace.

Nancy
Mudford

Q&A

What are your most popular
products or services?
Dermalogica skin care, Jane Iredale
mineral makeup, OPI nail polish, Footlogix
foot care, and Canadian-made, all
natural body care by Principessa.

What tip would you give women
who are starting a business?
Be driven to become profitable, be focused
on your goals and be patient. Be aware
of what is working and what is not. Make
changes quickly when necessary.

What place inspires you and why?
Kingfisher Resort Spa where I can unwind,
relax and recharge my batteries.

What do you CRAVE?
Travelling to exotic destinations,
long vacations with no Internet.

LE PETIT SPA

4-3701 W Broadway, Vancouver, 604.224.4314
lepetitspa.ca, Twitter: @lepetitspa

Professional. Relaxing. Friendly.
Le Petit Spa is an award-winning neighbourhood day spa offering facial treatments, microdermabrasion, relaxation massage, waxing and nail services. Their staff strive for excellent customer service and provide top-notch technical work. After seven years in business, they understand customers' needs and ensure satisfaction. Their goal is results-oriented services and satisfied customers.

Blair Kaplan

 Q&A

What tip would you give women
who are starting a business?
Owning your own business evolves from
being a job to becoming your lifestyle. Make
sure that you are following your heart and
your passion will help you succeed.

What is your favourite part about
owning a small business?
I love the flexibility and developing strong
relationships with both my merchants and my
members while helping the community grow.

What do you CRAVE?
Cheesecake and a community that wants
to try new activities to open up their eyes
and mind to live a fun and healthy life.

LIVING FREE CANADA

604.568.3733
livingfreecanada.com, Twitter: @LivingFreeCND

Innovative. Healthy. Motivating.
Living Free Canada (LFC) is Canada's online health and wellness community partnered with fun and healthy companies to provide you with elite coupons. LFC's goal is to encourage people to live their passions and enhance their lifestyle by creating awareness of life's exciting opportunities. You can print off coupons and have an active mind, happy heart and loving soul.

Explore Living Free Canada
@ www.livingfreecanada.com

604.568.3733   604.568.3733
info@livingfreecanada.com

Photos by Blue Olive Photography except portrait and top photo (opposite page) by Photography by Wade Andrew

Q&A

What are your most popular products or services?
Daily dog walking services—both private daily walks and group outings to the beaches or woods plus our loving, overnight in-home dog care while owners are away on vacation.

Who is your role model or mentor?
Mark Beckloff and Dan Dye, the founders of Three Dog Bakery. They created a business around their love for their own dogs, and we are working to emulate that too!

What place inspires you and why?
Hood River, Oregon. We love it there because it is so dog-friendly! The Old Columbia Scenic Highway is closed to motor traffic. It's an outdoor doggy paradise.

Tammy Preast and Shelly Dueck

LOVE ON A LEASH
TRUSTED DOG
CARE SERVICES

778.552.1301
loveonaleash.ca, Twitter: @loveonaleashbc

Experienced. Reliable. Nurturing.
Founded in 2008 by sisters Tammy Preast and Shelly Dueck, Love on a
Leash Trusted Dog Care Services has built up a solid reputation as the
company to care for your pooch while you are away! All their caregivers
specialise in responsible, reliable and loving in-home care for your dog
365 days a year. Their motto: "Peace of mind and a happy pooch."

165

Main photo (this page) and bottom middle photo (opposite page) by Le Beast Photography, portrait (opposite page) by Jaime Kowal Photography, bottom left and right photos (opposite page) by David Niddrie Photography

LUNAPADS
INTERNATIONAL

604.681.9953
lunapads.com, Twitter: @lunapads

Progressive. Empowered. Celebratory.
Lunapads offers a unique collection of sustainable personal care
products for women, specialising in alternatives to disposable pads and
tampons. Lunapads are used by more than 100,000 women in 40 countries.
Thanks to them making the switch, one million disposable pads
and tampons are being diverted from landfills every month.

 # Q&A

What are your most popular products or services?
Lunapads washable menstrual pads and pantyliners, Lunapanties padded underwear, and the DivaCup menstrual cup. We also offer a great selection of accessories and other organic, reusable everyday household linens.

What tip would you give women who are starting a business?
Do something that you truly believe in. You'll need the motivation, as building a business can take years.

What is your favourite part about owning a small business?
Doing something that we feel is creating positive social and environmental change.

What is your biggest fear?
Never overcoming negative societal attitudes towards menstruation, and, by extension, our products.

Suzanne Siemens and
Madeleine Shaw

· PAGE FLAGS ·

Zing Paperie & Design photographed
by Go-Lucky Photography

What is your biggest fear?

" I would say coming to the end of my life without being able to say I ticked off everything on my bucket list. After all... we're alive to live, right? "

Nina Pousette of Nina Pousette,
REALTOR® and Chocolatier

LUSSO BABY

1037 Marine Drive, North Vancouver, 778.340.0648
lussobaby.ca, Twitter: @lussobaby

Stylish. Natural. Modern.
Lusso Baby is a boutique that offers discerning parents everything they
need for newborns to six-year-olds. Lusso features modern furniture
for the nursery, stylish international and local clothing brands for little
ones and eco-friendly toys. Lusso's handpicked selection of essentials
for feeding time, bath time and playtime are perfect, whether you are
shopping for your first baby or gifting for your favourite toddler.

Photos by Tracey Ayton Photography

Shima
Javadi

Q&A

What are your most popular products or services?
Our complimentary baby concierge service is designed to save parents time and connect them to local businesses, such as professional photographers to capture precious moments or a 3-D ultrasound clinic.

What is your favourite part about owning a small business?
The opportunity to provide our customers with options and knowledge to simplify their lives, especially through the most important role: parenthood.

Who is your role model or mentor?
Oprah Winfrey. Despite obstacles in her life, she pursued her dreams and became a very successful woman. Her success has allowed her to make positive changes in the world.

North Vancouver

Jennifer
Cummer

 Q&A

What tip would you give women
who are starting a business?
Ask questions! Many brave and successful
women work in the same field as you and have
come across similar hurdles and struggles.
Pick their brain and then follow your heart.

How do you relax?
I indulge! Great food and good wine in the
company of my most treasured people
can make any hard day melt away.

What place inspires you and why?
Rome! Everyone lives and loves to the
fullest, all the while looking so well
put together. It's a charismatic place.

What is your favorite part about
owning a small business?
The freedom to create and build
the best business I can. The
freedom of steering the ship.

LÜT BOUTIQUE

4219 Main St, Vancouver, 604.568.1188
lutboutique.com, Twitter: @lutboutique

Sleek. Alluring. Chic.
Lüt is a curated boutique of national and international brands satisfying the
fashion cravings of men and women looking for something different. They believe
in long-term wearability over disposable trends and in clothing that expresses
your own unique, beautiful style. Lüt encourages their clients to explore, play
and fall in love with collections that effortlessly take you from day to night.

LUXE BEAUTY LOUNGE & MOBILE SPA

123-1208 Homer St, Vancouver, 604.689.LUXE (5893)
luxebeautylounge.com, Twitter: @luxeyaletown

Fun. Playful. Feminine.
Luxe Beauty Lounge was created as a luxurious and playful place where women go to look and feel beautiful, all in a cozy, feminine environment. With a focus on quality over quantity, Luxe carries immaculate products, offers complimentary edible spa treats and provides personalized spa services in a one-on-one setting.

Photos by Melissa Gidney Photography

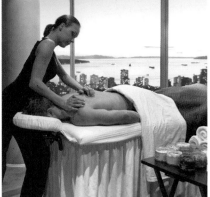

Catherine
Lalonde

 Q&A

What are your most popular
products or services?
Our amazing pedicures and mobile
service. Women love inviting girlfriends
over for an evening of great company,
food, wine and incredible spa services—
all in the comfort of their home!

Who is your role model or mentor?
My mom. I definitely credit her for instilling
me with a good work ethic, motivation and
values. She set the perfect example of what
a true, admirable woman should be.

What is your biggest fear?
Not having something to do. I like to keep busy!

What do you CRAVE?
Travelling to beautiful, exotic destinations.

Yaletown

Nicole Dennis Durnin

Q&A

What tip would you give women
who are starting a business?
Tell everyone you meet that you are starting a
business. You never know who you might run
into who can help you pursue your dream.

What is your favourite part about
owning a small business?
All the amazing and inspiring people
I meet every day: customers, vendors
and fellow entrepreneurs. I love it!

How do you relax?
Either a soothing facial at Skoah or a nice
dinner out with my husband and friends.

What place inspires you and why?
Italy. The people, the food, the history; their
way of life seems so carefree and relaxed. They
enjoy every day and take nothing for granted.

Photos by Melissa Gidney Photography except portrait by Ellen Ho of Hong Photography

Gastown

LYNNSTEVEN BOUTIQUE

225 Carrall St, Vancouver, 604.899.0808
lynnsteven.com, Twitter: @LYNNsteven

Edgy. Flirty. Progressive.
Among the vibrant boutiques and exciting restaurants of Vancouver's Gastown
lies LYNNsteven Boutique. Named after owner Nicole's mom and younger
brother, LYNNsteven is a reflection of Nicole's personal style—from fun
and flirty to edgier, fashion-forward pieces. You will find some of fashion's
hottest labels, such as McGinn, Son of John, Parker and Gorjana, plus
exciting Canadian designers such as Nicole Bridger and TOODLEBUNNY.

177

Christine
Kardum

Q&A

What are your most popular
products or services?
Our ability to work with small, challenging
downtown condominiums by transforming them
into spacious, efficient environments. The
talent to see beyond what you know you want.

Who is your role model or mentor?
My sister. There's no one else who can
make me feel like I can conquer the world
in a five-minute phone conversation.

What is your biggest fear?
A world without choices.

What is your motto or theme song?
Seamless detail should go unnoticed.

What place inspires you and why?
Paris. The architecture, the fashion,
the food... need I say more?

MAZA
INTERIOR DESIGN

604.417.6681
mazadesign.ca

Chic. Creative. Innovative.
Maza Interior Design brings exclusive, personalized style and service to each project. They take the time to listen to their clients' needs and aesthetic desires, delivering a polished design. Maza will transform your place into a stylish space where you can live, work or just be. They bring vision to reality, designing projects from casual to couture.

Photos by Bopomo Pictures, except main photo (this page) and top middle photo (opposite page) by Peter Taylor

MELISSA GIDNEY PHOTOGRAPHY

778.388.8805
mgimages.ca, melissagidneyblog.com

Passionate. Inspired. Genuine.
"I've already lived such an amazing life, and yet I feel it is just beginning," Melissa Gidney shares. Inspired by the moments in between and the simple things we overlook, Melissa strives to capture and create memories that will last a lifetime. "It's the love stories and laughter, the surprises and sentiment that make my job incredibly rewarding each and every day."

Melissa Gidney

Q&A

What are your most popular products or services?
Lifestyle sessions and wedding packages.

What tip would you give women who are starting a business?
The only thing that will limit you is yourself, so dream big!

What is your favourite part about owning a small business?
The freedom and power to create an amazing life... and meeting such incredible people every day!

What is your motto or theme song?
Dream your life, live your dream.

How do you relax?
It usually involves a glass of wine and good people, but moreso, just taking time to appreciate everything that surrounds me. Gratitude is calming.

Rebecca Troelstra

Q&A

What are your most popular products or services?
Hors d'oeuvres parties, signature cocktails and private dinners. Our café is the best kept-secret in Langley.

What is your favourite part about owning a small business?
Being able to constantly improve what I am offering is one of my favourite things. I love that I can set the bar higher every day.

Who is your role model or mentor?
Allison Awerbuch, vice president of Abigail Kirsch Catering in New York. She has invested in me and shown me that I can accomplish anything.

What place inspires you and why?
Spain. I grew up there and it is still dear to my heart. The food is all about love, and I try every day to recreate that in my kitchen.

MIZUNA CULINARY

20385 64th Ave, Langley, 778.888.4067
mizuna.ca, Twitter: @MizunaCulinary

Elegant. Colourful. Personal.
Mizuna Culinary is a catering company that offers personalized culinary services throughout the Lower Mainland. They strive to create food made from scratch, seasonal and sustainable while at the same time beautiful, colourful and delicious. Mizuna Culinary personally tailors every event to suit your needs while offering an undeniably outstanding atmosphere.

Photos by Trace Ayton Photography

MODUS PAPERIE & PRESS

604.313.6954
moduspress.com

Playful. Tactile. Enchanting.
Modus Paperie & Press is a boutique design and letterpress studio that specialises in traditional social stationery with a modern, playful twist. All Modus products are handprinted on a century-old letterpress where an inked image is pressed into soft paper, creating an impression you can see and feel. Ever mindful of the environment, Modus Paperie & Press is dedicated to using eco-friendly printing practices.

Photos by Candice Albach

Designer
MANNA WESCOTT
for

mōdus
PAPERIE & PRESS

Manna
Wescott

 Q&A

What are your most popular
products or services?
Our playful greeting cards, custom
wedding invitations and introduction
to letterpress workshops.

What tip would you give women
who are starting a business?
Genuine enthusiasm is infectious—
show everyone how excited you
are about what you do!

How do you relax?
I sit with a cup of tea and write lists. With a
million things on my mind, I've found the more
organized I am, the more relaxed I am.

What do you CRAVE?
I crave travelling to places where I will
be completely out of my element and
surrounded by total chaos, yet in my
everyday life I crave order and simplicity.

Q&A

What are your most popular
products or services?
Our clients love the food sensitivity testing. It
is a non-invasive, safe, pain-free and highly
developed method of determining imbalances
in the body. It takes the guesswork out!

What tip would you give women
who are starting a business?
Create a second-to-none support system. I
highly suggest finding mentors, creating a library
of books on business and collaborating with like-
minded women. This will help keep you sane!

What motivates you on a daily basis?
Seeing people's groceries and health statistics
keeps me motivated to spread the importance
of eating well. I know I have a lot of amazing
information to share with the world.

Jennifer Trecartin

MY EDIBLE ADVICE

604.313.2360
myedibleadvice.com, Twitter: @MyEdibleAdvice

Vibrant. Holistic. Educational.
My Edible Advice provides nutritional consulting, empowering people
to feel better one bite at a time. Getting on track with a personalized
nutrition program is fundamental for vitality and vibrancy. A program
is formulated to give you the tools you need to improve your nutritional
status. Specialising in computerized food sensitivity testing, you will
discover which foods fuel your body with optimal wellness.

NANNIES ON CALL

604.734.1776
nanniesoncall.com, Twitter: @nanniesoncall

Extraordinary. Efficient. Creative.
Nannies on Call is a bicoastal boutique agency headquartered in Vancouver since 2001, with an East Coast head office in Toronto and branches in Calgary, Whistler and Victoria. The company counts more than 400 nannies. Nannies on Call provides on call, full-time, part-time and short-term childcare placements at an unmatched standard of quality and reliability for prestigious hotels, film industry clients and private families.

Michelle Kelsey

 Q&A

What are your most popular
products or services?
On-call booking is our most popular service.
Families can book extraordinary nannies
24 hours a day, seven days a week!

Who is your role model or mentor?
My dad. He's been incredibly successful
building a number of different businesses. I feel
very lucky to have been able to learn from him.

How do you relax?
Dinner with my husband—he's a great cook!

What place inspires you and why?
I have a cabin out on a lake north of Squamish.
There's no electricity, no email (we actually have
to use an outhouse!)—I can hear myself think.

What do you CRAVE?
A spa weekend!

NICOLE GINSBERG JEWELRY

nicoleginsbergjewelry.blogspot.com

Chic. Charming. Feminine.
Nicole Ginsberg Jewelry is designed and created in Vancouver, featuring
high-quality contemporary designs made with 14-karat gold, sterling
silver and semi-precious stones. The line appeals to women of all ages
who crave timeless, unique and interesting jewellery that will become
signature pieces and will stay with them for years to come. Nicole
Ginsberg Jewelry can be found at various boutiques across Canada.

Nicole
Ginsberg

Q&A

What are your most popular products or services?
The charm necklaces and heirloom lockets have been extremely popular, as well as the unique chandelier and drop earrings with semi-precious stones. Also, custom designs for weddings and special events.

What tip would you give women who are starting a business?
What I have learned so far is to listen to what your instincts are telling you and seek out what brings you joy. Also, the ability to multitask is golden.

Who is your role model or mentor?
My two-year-old son's ability to find beauty, fun and wonder in the mundane has been very powerful to me, as has been my parents' fearlessness and perseverance.

nicole ginsberg jewelry
nicoleginsberg@hotmail.com
nicoleginsbergjewelry.blogspot.com

Q&A

What are your most popular products or services?
The most important service I can offer clients is a listening ear. In my line of work, the more I hear my clients, the better I can serve their needs.

What is your biggest fear?
I would say coming to the end of my life without being able to say I ticked off everything on my bucket list. After all... we're alive to *live*, right?

What is your motto or theme song?
"Courage atrophies from lack of use." Basically, if you want something badly enough, go get it... and it won't be easy!

What place inspires you and why?
My fiancé is from Brazil. The first time I visited, I was amazed by the warmth and joy of the people. They love and accept you just for being human!

Nina Pousette

NINA POUSETTE
REALTOR® AND CHOCOLATIER

778.994.6654
chocolaterealestateagent.com, Twitter: @RE_OnMyPlate

Urban. Fun. Gourmet.
Coined "The Chocolate Real Estate Agent," Nina works with RE/MAX Select Properties in Vancouver's west side and prides herself in working with women to achieve their real estate goals. Having lived in Paris for three years to train in the art of chocolate, she also tempts with her exclusive chocolate line, My Chocolate Tree, that only select few are fortunate enough to enjoy!

NOIR LASH LOUNGE

1150 Hamilton St, Vancouver, 604.915.LASH (5274)
3065 Granville St, Vancouver, 604.738.LASH (5274)
106-15745 Croydon Drive, Surrey, 604.531.7787
noirlashlounge.com, Twitter: @noirlashlounge

Flirty. Fresh. Fabulous.
Carrying the largest range of lashes in Canada with more than 100 different
styles to choose from, Noir Lash Lounge is Canada's first exclusive lashes-only
lounge. Technicians apply single, individual lashes to your own natural eyelash
using a special adhesive. Noir offers glamour in about an hour. Whether a Yummy
Mummy or an Addict for the Dramatic, the result is flirty, fresh and fabulous!

Photos by Ellen Ho of Hong Photography, except top middle photo, opposite page by Joel Dufresne and portrait by Go_Lucky Photography

Joyce Poon

 # Q&A

What are your most popular products or services?
Here at Noir, lash extensions aren't just an added service, it's our only service.

What is your favourite part about owning a small business?
Watching the visions in my head come to life. It's like watching my favourite book come to life on the silver screen—only this isn't a movie. It's real.

Who is your role model or mentor?
Judy Brooks, co-founder of Blo Blow Dry Bar and Irene Lee, founder of Pure Nail Bar,—both women with great business minds.

What is your motto or theme song?
"Only those who will risk going too far can possibly find out how far one can go."—T. S. Eliot. Still risking it...

Vi and Priscilla Phan

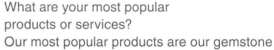 Q&A

What are your most popular
products or services?
Our most popular products are our gemstone
jewellery, photo art jewellery and vintage
cameos. We also host parties for artists who
are launching a new line for a new season.

What tip would you give women
who are starting a business?
Step out of your comfort zone and don't be
afraid to get a little crazy. Being innovative
is the key to obtaining results and important
information about growing your business.

What is your favourite part about
owning a small business?
The opportunities! We are grateful to have
the opportunity to meet and work with
artists who are genuinely passionate about
their work. It definitely rubs off on us!

OHKUOL

2439 Granville St, Vancouver, 604.732.6600
ohkuol.com, Twitter: @OhKuol

Creative. Chic. Edgy.
Allow OhKuol [oh-kool] to arouse your inner artist. A hidden gem nestled among the art galleries of South Granville, OhKuol features a wide array of locally made jewellery, handbags and one-of-a-kind accessories. Since opening in 2008, OhKuol specialises in finding local talent in Canada, especially Vancouver, bringing fashionistas the most chic and trendy jewellery pieces.

South Granville

Photos by Candice Albach

OLIVER & LILLY'S

1520 W 13th Ave, Vancouver, 604.736.7774
oliverandlillys.blogspot.com, Twitter: @OliverandLillys

Approachable. Refreshing. Fun.
Nestled comfortably around the corner from the South Granville
strip, Oliver & Lilly's is a delightful little shop for women to find
everything from T-shirts and knits to dresses and denim. The store is
welcoming, relaxed and simply a fun place to fill your wardrobe.

Photos by Candice Albach

Leighann Boquist

Q&A

What are your most popular
products or services?
Our denim and dresses are always the first
to go. Plus, our lemonade that we serve on
the weekends is devoured just as fast!

What is your favourite part about
owning a small business?
I love all the fabulous people I'm meeting along
the way, and being part of a community that
sees the value in local independent businesses.

Who is your role model or mentor?
When I grow up, I want to be Meryl Streep.

What place inspires you and why?
Travelling inspires me. I love venturing around
to find places off the beaten path, like little
quaint restaurants and flower shops. It's
always exciting to find a $2 taco joint!

199

Jillian Crago
and Kristy Rogerson

 Q&A

What is your favourite part about
owning a small business?
Having creative freedom in all facets of our
careers, from building our own schedule to
designing our branding and being responsible
for how the world views our company.

Who is your role model or mentor?
There are many strong, successful women who
have influenced us in different ways: in business,
fashion, personally and through inspiring us
to continue on our entrepreneurial path.

What motivates you on a daily basis?
Knowing that we are not only improving
women's style but their quality of life. Seeing
our clients' faces light up when they feel
confident in themselves is the biggest reward.

What is your motto or theme song?
When you look good, you feel good.

OPERATION STYLE

operationstyle.ca, Twitter: @operationstyle

Fresh. Confident. Innovative.
Personal styling company Operation Style believes that style is in what
you say, what you do and how you live. Sometimes it's an appearance or
an attitude. Style is the essence of your being. It accentuates, defines and
conceals. At its best, style reflects the soul. Operation Style's commitment
to clients guides them on their journey to define their true style.

OWN THE ROOM

604.926.3225
owntheroom.ca, Twitter: @taajakayler

Transformational. Graceful. Empowered.
Taaja Kayler has built on her experience as a professional model and created a unique and personal empowerment business: OWN THE ROOM. In her fun and interactive classes, she provides all women the opportunity to transform themselves, and be more graceful and confident in their personal and professional lives. On her portable red carpet, she teaches The Walk, The Look and what it takes to Own the Room.

Taaja
Kayler

Q&A

What is your favourite part about owning a small business?
I want to grow and my business challenges me on all levels to do that. I enjoy the flexibility, variety and the people I meet and work with and their creations.

What is your biggest fear?
Being overwhelmed or stuck. Sometimes you just have to give a big scream and ta-da! A new door opens and you're off again... someone heard and answered the call!

How do you relax?
A seawall walk with a girlfriend, culminating at Crema's for a cappuccino and fun chatter!

What place inspires you and why?
The beach. I give it all away and the answers come back to me through the sounds of the crackling, foaming waves. I write profusely.

PAINTED LIGHTHOUSE
COUNSELLING & CONSULTING

604.842.2427
paintedlighthouse.com

Playful. Reflective. Compassionate.
Courtney and Rebecca are experienced registered clinical counsellors
with specialty areas in early childhood and special needs therapy. Painted
Lighthouse Counselling & Consulting offers a safe place to strengthen family
relationships. Their knowledge and enthusiasm help guide parents to become
more connected and in sync with their children, bringing balance and satisfaction
to their role as a parent. Services are available to families and corporations.

Rebecca Mitchell and
Courtney Nichols

 Q&A

What are your most popular
products or services?
A wide range of therapeutic services are
offered, including improving communication and
coping skills in families dealing with transitions,
mental health concerns (anxiety/depression)
and a specialty focus in treatment for autism.

What motivates you on a daily basis?
Our passion is the children—seeing them laugh,
play and smile when they are experiencing
authentic moments with their parents!

What is your motto or theme song?
"Here Comes the Sun" by the Beatles.

What do you CRAVE?
Learning experiences in the ever-evolving field
of mental health to challenge ourselves and
continually grow. Genuine moments connecting
with the people we love, usually with wine!

Crissy Giesbrecht

Q&A

What are your most popular products or services?
Our custom "boarding pass" invitations are popular with couples having destination weddings. Fun, unique and far from typical; people love receiving these invitations in the mail!

What tip would you give women who are starting a business?
Trust your instincts. And don't underestimate your time—things have a way of always taking longer than you think they will.

What is your motto or theme song?
Everything happens for a reason.

What place inspires you and why?
Europe. I love everything about it—the art, architecture, landscape, food, the people. I'm most inspired when I'm riding on a train somewhere in Europe.

✳ PAR AVION DESIGN

778.317.5990
paraviondesign.com

Creative. Distinct. Inspired.
Par avion design is a boutique invitation studio that offers fresh and unique invitations, announcements and stationery. Custom designs range from classic to modern, minimalist to bold; the attention to detail and use of only the finest quality materials are unmistakable. They'll work with you, on your budget, to create a fabulous custom design that will reflect your unique personality, style and vision.

Photos by Crissy Giesbrecht, except portrait by Dan Denker

Zuka Artful Accessories photographed
by Go-Lucky Photography

What tip would you give women who are starting a business?

" *Ask questions! Many brave and successful women work in the same field as you and have come across similar hurdles and struggles. Pick their brain and then follow your heart.* "

Jennifer Cummer of Lüt Boutique

PEBBLE

2675 Arbutus St (at W 11th Ave), Vancouver, 604.568.6923
pebblebaby.com, Twitter: @pebblebabystore

Playful. Earth-friendly. Creative.
Owner Jordan Proulx left the corporate world in 2008 to open Pebble with
a vision to create a baby and children's store wholly devoted to conscious
living—a "lifestyle store for kids." It's the ideal place to find a unique
array of styles from small, independent local designers as well as natural
and organic products of the highest quality from all over the world.

Photos by Tracey Ayton Photography

Jordan Tomas Proulx

Q&A

What tip would you give women
who are starting a business?
Don't talk yourself out of what
you're meant to do.

What is your favourite part about
owning a small business?
I love being responsible for my own
successes and failures. There's
something very liberating about that.

What motivates you on a daily basis?
I'm motivated by lots of things but mostly by my
son. I want to teach him through my example to
challenge and apply himself in all his pursuits.

What is your motto or theme song?
"Make it happen." I mostly say it to myself,
as opposed to barking it to others! It's
a motivator—anything is possible if
you're focused and determined.

Kitsilano

Traci Costa

Q&A

What are your most popular products or services?
Every season we have a piece that is four-in-one—it's a dress, a top, tunic or skirt (and it's reversible too). Who wouldn't love so many options!

What motivates you on a daily basis?
I want to work hard for my children so they understand that life is what you make it. My team inspires me to work hard every day.

What place inspires you and why?
Coffee shops have always been a great place for me to work and think. I love the activity and the hussle and bussle; I have had many aha! moments!

What do you CRAVE?
A world where all children can play.

PEEKABOO BEANS

604.279.BEAN (2326)
peekaboobeans.com, Twitter: @peekaboobeans

Playful. Stylish. Progressive.
Peekaboo Beans offers adorable and durable duds—a perfect combination of style and comfort for kids who fancy themselves playground professionals. Versatile pieces slip on and off with ease and have loads of fun features too. All items are prewashed so no surprises, and styles are mix-and-match for Daddy-proof dressing. Playtime never looked so good! Peekaboo Beans provides ingredients for a playful life!

213

Rocio Garcia

 Q&A

What are your most popular products or services?
Our classic jeans in dark night blue and black washes.

What is your favourite part about owning a small business?
Being able to carve my own road to success doing something I love with the help of my family.

What motivates you on a daily basis?
I have a burning desire to produce a superior pair of jeans and I care about what I produce because it is a reflection of my personal character and integrity.

What is your motto or theme song?
I am obsessed with great design and excellent craftsmanship, so much so that I would argue that one cannot exist without the other.

THE QUEEN OF JEANS

778.297.1372
thequeenofjeans.com, Twitter: @thequeenofjeans

Fashionable. Unique. Quality.
The Queen of Jeans is a fabulous young company committed to the design
and manufacture of form-fitting, high-quality jeans that flatter women's bodies.
Paying special attention to details and design, every pair of jeans is unique.
Achieving perfect balance between comfort, fit and style, they are a must-
have item in any woman's closet and a designer piece that women crave.

Photos by Bopomo Pictures.

ROUGE
MAKE-UP LOUNGE

1038 Hamilton St, Vancouver, 604.681.1118
rougemakeuplounge.com

Unique. Chic. Vibrant.
Rouge Make-Up Lounge is a premier, high-end makeup lounge offering a posh,
intimate space for women to indulge in relaxing makeovers and consultations
with trained professionals. Unlike department store cosmetic stands, Rouge
offers personalised services in a tranquil, pressure-free environment.

Photos by Melissa Gidney Photography

Pegah Vajdi

 # Q&A

**What tip would you give women
who are starting a business?**
Start with what is right rather than what
is acceptable. Follow your dreams. Being
bold is genius, powerful and magical.

**What is your favourite part about
owning a small business?**
I enjoy getting to know my clients and
creating an atmosphere that is welcoming
for every individual. Seeing happy clients
makes me love my job even more.

Who is your role model or mentor?
My role model is my father because he
has raised me to be the person I am
today and has always believed in me.

How do you relax?
Walking by the seawall, not thinking about
anything except my goals and aspirations.

Yaletown

SABAI THAI SPA

571 Cardero St, Vancouver, 604.568.6227
3B-987 Marine Drive, North Vancouver, 604.985.8896
thaispa.ca, Twitter: @SabaiThai

Warm. Professional. Authentic.
Sabai Thai Spa is an exclusive boutique spa with two unique locations offering clients the highest-quality massage and organic skin care products. It is Sabai Thai Spa's goal for every guest to leave with memorable experiences, feeling cared for, relaxed, healthy and happy with how they look and feel—every time they visit!

Q&A

Neata
Goutier

What are your most popular products or services?
For the athlete or weekend warrior, the traditional thai massage; for calm, comfort and aromatherapy, Thai herbal compress massage. Eminence Organic Skin Care products sell like hotcakes!

What tip would you give women who are starting a business?
Focus on your goal, keep a realistic mind, and figure out how to work smarter not harder. Keep your dreams close to your heart. Don't give up and trust you will succeed.

What motivates you on a daily basis?
My staff. They are so amazing—truly dedicated, hard working, caring and sincere. Their laughter and smiles on a long day really keep me going.

Erin Shum

Q&A

What are your most popular products or services?
The classic mani-pedi combo. A relaxing service that includes a scented soak, organic sugar scrub, lotion massage and polish application with a take-home file and orangewood stick!

What is your favourite part about owning a small business?
I get to meet so many wonderful people on a daily basis—from mothers and their beautiful girls to wise older ladies, to excited grads and career women.

Who is your role model or mentor?
My mom. She is the one woman who grounds me, makes me laugh and cry at the same time, and gives me honest feedback as I continue building myself.

What is your motto or theme song?
Eat well, dress well and sleep lots!

She to Shic
boutique beauty lounge
604.269.3003

where beauty meets convenience... naturally

SHE TO SHIC
BOUTIQUE BEAUTY LOUNGE

2315 W 41st Ave, Vancouver, 604.269.3003
shetoshic.com, Twitter: @shetoshic

Luxurious. Convenient. Chic.
She to Shic Boutique Beauty Lounge is the first green nail, hair and lash lounge in the prestigious Kerrisdale neighbourhood. Winners of the 2009 Interior Design Institute of BC's Retail Award, this lounge is dedicated to being environmentally friendly, from design and construction to products and services. They offer an ethical beauty experience at an affordable price, without sacrificing the quality, luxury or atmosphere of their treatments.

Kerrisdale

SIMPLY FRENCH CAFE

3742 W 10th Ave, Vancouver, 604.568.6180

Cosmopolitan. Artistic. Welcoming.
Simply French Cafe has a stylish, friendly atmosphere. Enjoy delicious
coffee and tea and a wonderful selection of freshly baked goods, delicious
croissants, macarons, scrumptious cakes, cookies, brownies, muffins, lemon
bars and handmade truffles. Simply French also has a great selection of
wholesome paninis, salads, soups and daily specials that make it a great spot
to meet for lunch. They also offer beautiful gifts from all over the world!

Musée d'Orsay →

CHILDREN'S
MENU

GRILLED CHEESE   3.25

NUTELLA SANDWICH   3.25

HOT CHOCOLATE FLUFFY 2.25

VANILLA STEAMED MILK 2.00

Photos by Candice Albach

Isobel Drummond with her daughter, Sara-Peri

 Q&A

What are your most popular products or services?
Baked goods made on the premises with all-natural ingredients and free of preservatives, paninis, soups, salads, coffee and tea, silk scarves, candles and jewellery.

What is your favourite part about owning a small business?
The independence. I love being able to experiment and try new things. Not being part of a corporate chain allows me the freedom to grow organically and take risks.

What place inspires you and why?
France. Every region has its own charm and beauty. The food, the wine... And Paris is just so beautiful. I will live there one day!

West Point Grey

Tazeem
Jamal

Q&A

What is your favourite part about
owning a small business?
The freedom to make my own lifestyle
and work as hard as I desire!

Who is your role model or mentor?
My mom, Nazira. She has always been
my biggest fan and my inspiration!

What motivates you on a daily basis?
The desire for variety and the drive to learn
new things are my obsession. Skindulgence is
one of five different businesses that I operate!

What do you CRAVE?
Our signature lavender peppermint
tea, good dark chocolate and romantic
escapes with my husband!

SKINDULGENCE
THE URBAN RETREAT

254A Newport Drive, Port Moody, 604.469.2688
skindulgencespa.com

Sophisticated. Timeless. Nurturing.
Skindulgence is a boutique spa, where for more than 20 years client relationships
have been built on trust and integrity. As the name suggests, Skindulgence is
passionate about skincare. They offer age management solutions, with results-
oriented services and products including cutting-edge nutricosmetics indigestible
skincare. Unlike most spas, the Skindulgence facial menu boasts more than 25
different skincare treatments. Be prepared to exhale and leave with glorious skin!

Photos by Jordana Dhahan of Through the Looking Glass Photography, except portrait

SKN HOLISTIC REJUVENATION CLINIC

150-1152 Mainland St, Yaletown, 604.568.6333
sknclinic.ca, Twitter: @SKNClinic

Revitalizing. Calm. Transformational.
SKN Holistic Rejuvenation Clinic is a peaceful, hidden oasis where clients go
to rejuvenate their mind, body and spirit. SKN combines the western world of
medical esthetics together with eastern medicine to help clients achieve beautiful
skin and great health. The range of non-invasive procedures offered at SKN
is truly powerful and unique. SKN Clinic is located in beautiful Yaletown.

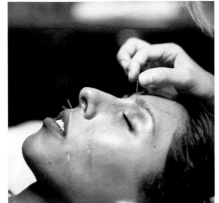

Amanda
Beisel

 Q&A

What are your most popular
products or services?
Cosmetic acupuncture, customized
peels and osmosis medical facials.

What tip would you give women
who are starting a business?
Don't let fear hold you back. Be
fierce and be determined.

Who is your role model or mentor?
Heather White is my mentor. She has been
my business coach from day one and
continues to guide me in the right direction.

What place inspires you and why?
Yaletown inspires me because it is full
of successful female entrepreneurs. It is
really incredible to see so many women-
owned businesses in such a small area.

Photos by Candice Albach

THE SMARTY PANTS GIFT COMPANY LTD.

604.263.2642
smartassgifts.com, Twitter: @smartassgifts

Fun. Flirty. Fabulous.
With a sassy backside and inspirational custom-printed gusset, Smart Ass
undies say they provide a panty pep talk with every pair, and they deliver!
Smart Ass skinny skivvies are beautifully packaged and ready for gift giving,
but don't give them all away because they're also perfect for everyday wear.
Visit smartassgifts.com for a list of retailers who stock Smart Ass girly gear.

Carla Gilley

Q&A

What tip would you give women who are starting a business?
Keep calm and carry on. Listen to your instincts. Get out there and network. You'll be amazed how generous fellow entrepreneurs are with their time, advice and support.

Who is your role model or mentor?
Ritz from I Love My Muff taught me to be fearless and not to apologize. Diane of Diane's Lingerie has been successful for so many years and keeps getting better.

What motivates you on a daily basis?
Success. Happy clients and customers. Fans who love our products keep me going. The excitement of introducing new colours, sayings and products motivates me.

What place inspires you and why?
Spanish Banks at low tide, surrounded by the beauty of the city and nature: a place where possibilities seem infinite.

Nancy Mudford

Q&A

What are your most popular
products or services?
Jane Iredale minerals, Dermalogica, Guinot and
Phytomer are our best-selling skin care brands.
We have an amazing selection of nail polish
collections, ranging from OPI to China Glaze.

What tip would you give women
who are starting a business?
Be innovative and figure out how you
are different from your competition.

What is your motto or theme song?
Don't be afraid to make mistakes.
It's the only way you grow.

What place inspires you and why?
Whistler—beautiful mountains, incredible
views from the top, fun atmosphere
and relaxed people; lots of sports
to do in all seasons as well.

SPA BOUTIQUE

3630 W 4th Ave, Vancouver, 877.224.4315, 604.734.0943
spaboutique.ca, Twitter: @spaboutique

Luxurious. Informative. Dynamic.
Spa Boutique offers a unique selection of professional skin care, makeup, nail
and hair products. Only the best results-oriented product lines are brought on,
and new lines are always being sourced. They deliver anywhere in Canada, so
your favourite beauty products can be in your hands as quickly as possible.

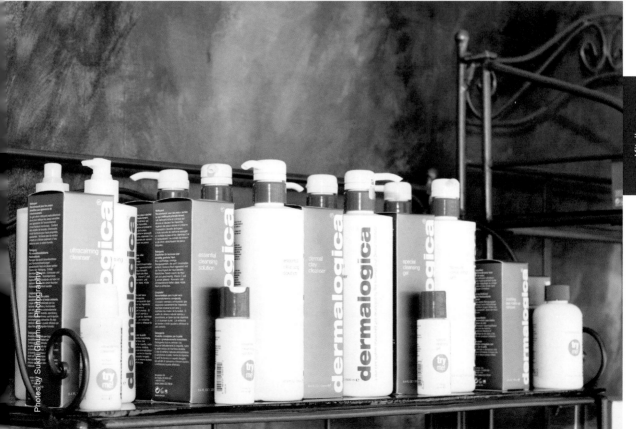

Photos by Sukhi Ghuman Photography

Kitsilano

Mika Livingston

Q & A

What are your most popular
products or services?
People love our individually packaged, custom-
decorated cookies as favours or gifts... and
call us at all hours to order our Grandma
Nam's Classic Chocolate Chip Cookies!

What tip would you give women
who are starting a business?
Do what you love, and do it as well as you can.

What is your favourite part about
owning a small business?
It gives me a creative outlet... every custom
order is an exciting challenge, and I love it
when we create beautiful new cookies.

What motivates you on a daily basis?
The excitement of happy customers!
I love making someone's cookie idea
become a delicious reality!

▼ THE STEVESTON COOKIE COMPANY

778.297.1597
thestevestoncookiecompany.com, Twitter: @StevestonCookie

Delicious. Stylish. Original.
The Steveston Cookie Company specialises in gorgeously decorated, melt-in-your-mouth delicious cookies for any occasion. From weddings to corporate gifts to informal book club gatherings, they have your event covered with cookies in any theme your heart desires. Owner Mika Livingston will ensure each cookie is stylish and perfect for your day. The Steveston Cookie Company is known for its attention to detail, fresh ingredients and original designs.

STONZ

604.568.6364
stonzwear.com, Twitter: @stonzwear

Functional. Innovative. Canadian-made.
Lisa Will could not find warm footwear that stayed on her six-month-old's feet when he was in a backpack. To remedy this, in 2004, Stonz booties were born. Since then, the line has expanded to include a range of durable children's wear with Hatz, Mittz, and Linerz for inside the Booties. After moving from Lisa's basement, and spilling into the garage, Stonz now makes all products in their Vancouver BC factory.

Photos by Sukhi Ghuman Photography except main photo (this page)

Lisa Will

 Q&A

What tip would you give women
who are starting a business?
You'll never work so hard, for so long, or
find something as challenging yet enjoyable
all at the same time, as entrepreneurship...
except perhaps being a mom.

What is your motto or theme song?
Attitude is everything.

How do you relax?
Truly I cannot. I've been told I am a
perfect candidate for yoga. The best
I can do is fish—sitting while being
productive all at the same time!

What do you CRAVE?
Time... to think, to envision, to lead, to be
with my kids and family, to be outdoors
and to build a company and culture
that employees love working for.

Photos by Melissa Gidney Photography

STRIPPED WAX BAR

1226 Hamilton St, Vancouver, 604.681.8660
getstripped.ca, Twitter: @StrippedWaxBar

Smooth. Professional. Efficient.
Catering to both ladies and gents, Stripped is an exclusive wax bar
that believes in no fuss, no frills and no unwanted hair. Hair removal
deserves as little of your time as possible, so their professional Strippers
will have you in and out in no time, feeling smooth and confident. Their
mantra is simple: remove hair, remove it well, remove it fast.

Susan Vu

Q&A

What is your favourite part about owning a small business?
It's so rewarding to see my vision come to life and see the customers who I've built the business around enjoy what I've created.

Who is your role model or mentor?
My greatest role models are my mother and sister. They've taught me what it is to be strong, independent, forward-thinking and fearless.

What motivates you on a daily basis?
My biggest motivator is opportunity. One thing will always lead to another, so you've got to try new things in order to know what other opportunities are out there.

What do you CRAVE?
Travel. Knowing there are countless amazing places around the world to see is what keeps me working so hard.

get stripped.

stripped
LADIES & GENTS WAX BAR

stripped

Yaletown

Julie Sperling

Q&A

What are your most popular
products or services?
I stumbled upon a few bolts of vintage Dick
& Jane fabrics in my ongoing search for
material. They always stir up happy nostalgia
in folks... definitely my best sellers!

What is your favourite part about
owning a small business?
What I put in is what I get out, which is perfect
with two young children at home. I'm in control.

What is your motto or theme song?
David Bowie always gets my blood
running. In a good way.

What place inspires you and why?
London. The history, the art, the fashion,
the people, the markets, the architecture,
the drink, the food, the streets, the
tubes, the parks, the shops...

SUPERFLY LULLABIES

superflylullabies.com, Twitter: @superflyjulie

Swank. Cute. Modern.
Superfly Lullabies are super-swank blankets to fit your lifestyle and your baby. Perfect for bedtime, tummy time or anytime: a great way to wrap up the babe you love, with love. Born of a desire to see more adult-friendly baby items on the market, Superfly Lullabies is continually striving to provide the hippest trends and styles that will pass the test of time.

SUPERFLY LULLABIES
SUPER-SWANK BLANKIES FOR YOUR SUPER-SWANK BABE.

TOTALLY BITCHIN NURSING COVER.

SUPERFLYLULLABIES.ETSY.COM
SUPERFLYLULLABIES@GMAIL.COM

TANDEM LANEHOUSE COMPANY

944 W 20th Ave, 604.568.6889
tandemlanehousecompany.com, Twitter: @tandemlanehouse

Urban. Chic. Versatile.
Along with her partners, Mandy Clark has built and furnished Vancouver's first
demonstration laneway home in her Douglas Park backyard. Tandem Lanehouse
Company (TLC) has developed a suite of lanehouse designs with multifunctional
uses to complement your main residence. TLC's team of architects and tradespeople
guides homeowners through the design build process, saving you time and money.

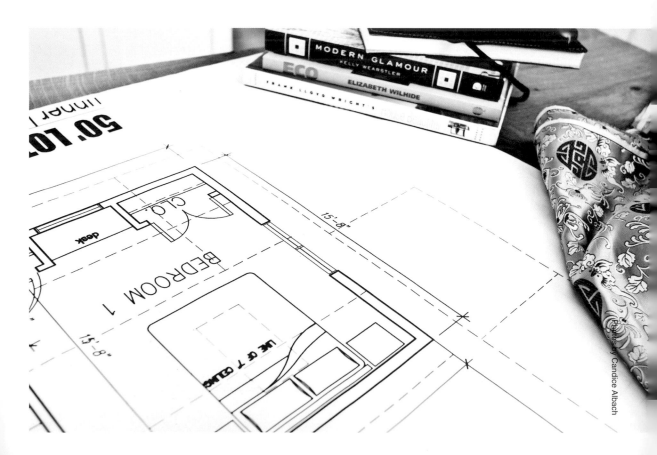

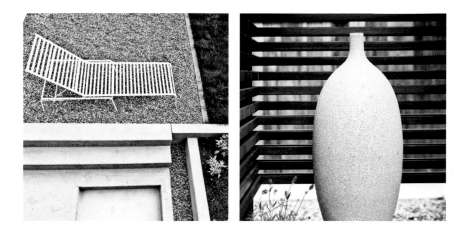

Mandy Clark

Q&A

What tip would you give women
who are starting a business?
Cement good habits early on and build
on them. The power is in your routine.
Surround yourself with people who will lift
you up and help you achieve your goals.

Who is your role model or mentor?
Shaf Shivji, owner of Dunbar Lumber,
Benjamin Moore Paints and the Local
Cafe. He has an incredible work ethic, an
unwavering commitment to his goals and
an extraordinary generosity of spirit.

What is your motto or theme song?
When I was 10 my father said, "Keep
your eye on the prize, swim your own
race and never get out of the pool."

What place inspires you and why?
Paris—the perfect composition of
traditional and modern style.

Kelly Strongitharm
and Desirée Dupuis

Q&A

What are your most popular
products or services?
Investment vehicles: RRSPs, tax-
free savings accounts, life insurance,
critical illness insurance, disability
insurance and group benefit plans.

What is your favourite part about
owning a small business?
Working with my best friend and knowing
that the sky's the limit. Together we know
that if we work hard enough we can
achieve everything we want in life.

Who is your role model or mentor?
Ivanka Trump. She is a classy, sophisticated,
smart and strong woman. Michael Bublé—
local boy whose success is directly
attributed to hard work and perseverance.
He is still remarkably humble.

☎ THREE SIXTY FINANCIAL GROUP

778 245 2262
threesixtyfg.ca, Twitter: @threesixtyfg

Smart. Sophisticated. Driven.
Three Sixty Financial Group is a boutique financial firm that helps young families, professionals and business owners plan and achieve all of their short- and long-term financial goals. Owners Kelly and Desirée are independent brokers who work for clients directly. They offer a fun, sophisticated approach to financial planning and work with responsible people who are ready to act on advice.

TRACEY AYTON PHOTOGRAPHY

604.738.5605
tphotography.ca

Airy. Beautiful. Fascinating.
With more than 15 years of photography experience, Tracey Ayton has created her own beautiful style, which is reflected in the pictures she takes. Her eye for detail is impeccable and her easygoing, creative and professional approach is what makes her clients feel at ease. She has established a strong hold in the business.

Tracey Ayton

Q&A

What are your most popular products or services?
My business caters to a few different type of clients: lifestyle, interiors, food and weddings. I'm fortunate that all of what I offer is popular. It's good to be a chameleon in photography. My Polaroid artwork has also been a favourite throughout the years. And, after numerous exhibitions and shows, my quirky images can now be found at Liberty on West Broadway.

What is your favourite part about owning a small business?
The people I meet, the places I go and the things I learn along the way. Nothing beats independence and freedom.

What do you CRAVE?
I crave New York City! The sights, the sounds, the energy and the shopping are like nothing else. Oh... and some of that Dutch Girl Chocolate I photographed on page 94!

Gail Conzatti

 # Q&A

What are your most popular
products or services?
KAIROS handbags, Gilmour, Carny Love,
Cecile Benac and Shi belt buckles.

What tip would you give women
who are starting a business?
You need a lot of passion and
a good business plan.

What is your favourite part about
owning a small business?
I love the variety of my day and
being able to change and adapt my
business to the market demands.

What is your motto or theme song?
Stay calm and carry on.

What place inspires you and why?
The outdoors. The quiet beauty,
the colours, the simplicity.

Photos by Jordana Dhahan of Through the Looking Glass Photography

TUTTA MIA

1302 Victoria Drive, Vancouver, 604.255.4177
tutta-mia.com

Refreshing. Stylish. Functional.
A gem in the East End of Vancouver, Tutta Mia attracts a strong following
from across the Lower Mainland. Known for their personalised service,
Canadian-made designs and great prices, Tutta Mia is a definite stop
on any shopping day and a destination when you are searching for the
perfect outfit. Tutta Mia also features an in-house line of clothing.

Alarte Silks photographed by Go-Lucky Photography

What tip would you give women
who are starting a business?

" *Just do it, but with your
eyes wide open. Know
that it is going to take
you more time and more
money than you ever
planned. But it's worth it!* "

Zahra Mamdani of Wear Else

UNION SECURITIES LTD.

900-700 W Georgia St, Vancouver, 604.691.2853
union-securities.com

Prosperous. Strategic. Customised.
With Union Securities Ltd., Member CIPF, Catherine offers her clients full-service investment services. She assists clients in building their own pension plans through retirement savings plans and tax-free savings accounts. She offers exceptional products and strategies, which provide annual results to her clients, in profits and cash dividends. Catherine also specialises in helping business owners with complete financial planning. Historically, she has assisted her clients in revamping their RRSPs, held within large banks and mutual fund companies, and turning them into profitable annual returns.

Catherine Jones

Q&A

What tip would you give women who are starting a business?
Don't let a man make you think he can do it better. Women are naturally more compassionate and intuitive, which can make us just as successful, if not more!

What is your favorite part about owning a small business?
Independence! I have the ability to control my own destiny. My success is what I make of it. And I can take a vacation at my leisure, without reporting to anyone!

What motivates you on a daily basis?
I'm a generous and compassionate person, which can also be a downfall, as many have taken advantage of me. So I live by the motto: "Success is the best revenge."

How do you relax?
Yoga, travelling and spending time with my family and friends.

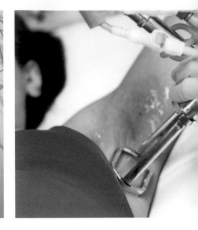

Janiece Wiens

 Q&A

What are your most popular
products or services?
The most popular service at UBL is hair
removal, combined with high-quality skin care
products. Clients are always coming back
for a fresh anti-aging treatment as well.

What tip would you give women
who are starting a business?
Business is an exciting yet nerve-
racking experience. A constant
understanding of the numbers as well as
a broad perspective in which to view your
accomplishments and failures are helpful.

What is your favourite part about
owning a small business?
The interactions with clients and the ability to
make the necessary changes to keep them
happy—these are a few things I enjoy the most.

URBAN BODY LASER

860-777 Hornby St, 604.696.5506
urbanbodylaser.com

Vibrant. Contemporary. Inspiring.
Urban Body Laser (UBL), established in 2004, offers expert laser hair removal
from professionally trained technicians. A visit to UBL begins with a warm smile
from the receptionist in a comforting environment. UBL is committed to the
highest standards and pledge compassionate, timely and confidential care.

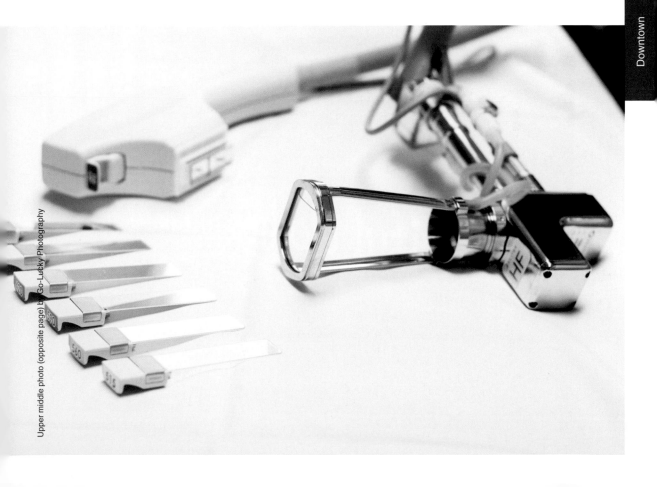

Upper middle photo (opposite page) by Go-Lucky Photography

URBANITY

2412 Granville St, Vancouver, 604.801.6262
urbanity.ca, Twitter: @myurbanity

Colourful. Well-made. Relaxed.
Julia moved from Denmark to Vancouver with the dream of starting a shop
selling clothing and accessories made by caring hands. Featuring the Norwegian
line OLEANA, she opened a shop that brought colour and passion to the
neighbourhood. Among the many unique items available, local textile artists are
also featured. URBANITY moved from Gastown to South Granville in May 2010.

Julia Manitius

 # Q&A

What tip would you give women who are starting a business?
Take a business course and make a realistic business plan. Before opening in a specific location, take time to learn if it is the right place for your product.

What is your motto or theme song?
My own motto is "make it happen; don't wait for it to happen."

How do you relax?
I relax by going to the theatre, going to my favourite restaurant, riding my bike and enjoying a massage. I also relax by exploring ways of marketing my business!

What place inspires you and why?
Copenhagen is a city for people. It is full of small shops that present their products in interesting and individual ways. People dare to explore new ideas and new places.

Jill Amery

Q&A

What are your most popular
products or services?
Contests, hip finds, recipes, kids quotes
and tools (menu planners, breast-feeding
logs, vaccination records). The MommyFit
contest, which launched in 2009, was a huge
success and drew quite a readership.

What motivates you on a daily basis?
The moms I see with vacant looks who
are close to tears. In our society we are
often prompted to cater to our children,
sometimes to the detriment of ourselves.

What place inspires you and why?
Paris. The citizens strive to master
their crafts and the resulting beauty is
appreciated by all—finials on a fence, the
opera chorus, the food in a farmhouse...

URBANMOMMIES

604.418.4800
urbanmommies.com, Twitter: @urbanmommies

Catchy. Fabulous. Intelligent.
UrbanMommies is like an online Canadian *Vogue* for pregnancy and parenting.
Using a youthful writing style, UrbanMommies engages readers with articles,
tips and information on all things belly, bambino and kid. Consumers find
unique products, easy recipes, articles and health and safety tips.

VANCOUVERMOM.CA

604.764.9177
vancouvermom.ca, Twitter: @vancouver_mom

Local. Intelligent. Unique.
Launched in October 2009, VancouverMom.ca is a hyper-local online
magazine that gives moms living in Metro Vancouver access to an intelligent,
beautiful and unique side of the city. Whether it's where to shop, where to
eat or what to do, VancouverMom.ca prides itself on uncovering hidden
local gems and publishing stories that appeal to urban-minded moms.

Christine Pilkington

 Q&A

What are your most popular products or services?
The VancouverMom.ca Reviewer Network, where moms write reviews of products and services; downloadable guides; giveaways for things like concert tickets and spa services; and articles about restaurants, shops and other hidden gems.

What motivates you on a daily basis?
I used to be about my career. Motherhood has shifted my priorities: I'm now motivated by my kids and having the freedom to spend time with them on my terms.

What is your motto or theme song?
Just go for it. Just start and then correct course along the way. Also, take calculated risks. All my success started from making intelligent wagers that have paid off.

vancouver mom.ca

www.vancouvermom.ca
contact@vancouvermom.ca

Twitter: vancouver_mom
Facebook: facebook.vancouvermom.ca

Jessica Elliott and
Deborah Richardson

 Q&A

What are your most popular
products or services?
All 70 lines we carry are stunning, but our
house lines Coral Moon and the Velvet Room
are specifically designed for our clientele.

What tip would you give women
who are starting a business?
Find a mentor, be open to change
and stay tuned to your intuition.

What is your favourite part about
owning a small business?
It allows for continuous learning,
creativity and personal growth.

How do you relax?
A mom and daughter power walk, sushi
lunch or simply sipping wine, sharing
ideas, laughing and being super silly.

THE VELVET ROOM BOUTIQUE

2248 W 41st Ave, Vancouver, 604.264.8664
thevelvetroomboutique.com, Twitter: @the_velvetroom

Exclusive. Eclectic. Chic.
The Velvet Room Boutique is an extensive collection of the finest
Canadian-made fashions and accessories. Mother and daughter duo,
Deborah Richardson and Jessica Elliott bring a personal approach to
celebrating every woman's style. Founded on the philosophy that true
style is ageless, the collection is selected to combine classic looks with
a twist, signature pieces and unique high-fashion accessories.

Photos by Candice Albach

Kerrisdale

VERVE HAIR LOUNGE

227 Lonsdale Ave, North Vancouver, 778.340.4654
vervehairlounge.com, Twitter: @vervehair

Creative. Inspired. Gracious.
Verve Hair Lounge is an award-winning, eco-conscious hair salon and art
gallery. With support from brands Shu Uemura and Redken, the Verve stylist
believes in hair as art. This team of driven individuals brings a unique blend
of talent, ambition and service to the North Shore. It is the salon of choice for
many locals and a destination for clients from Whistler to the Lower Mainland.

Amber George

Q&A

What tip would you give women who are starting a business?
Believe in your vision. Write a plan and stick to it. When it no longer makes sense, be flexible. Maintain your vision. Act with integrity. Get your sleep.

What is your favourite part about owning a small business?
I love creating the vision. I love the ever-changing landscape. Watching the growth and seeing the potential, in myself, my business and my team. I love going to work.

What is your motto or theme song?
"Others have seen what is and asked why. I have seen what could be and asked why not."—Pablo Picasso

What do you CRAVE?
I crave a life that I can say was full of life, love, experiences and laughter. A creative life. An adventurous life.

North Vancouver

VINCENT PARK

4278 Main St, Vancouver, 604.879.6665
vincentpark.ca, Twitter: @vincentpark

Fashion-forward. Thoughtful. Edgy.
Sisters Lauren and Cara Stryer opened Vincent Park two years ago in a space that
previously housed an antique store. The lofty space stays true to its retro roots
with heirlooms like a 1960s photo booth, vintage maps and antique chandeliers.
Vincent Park is thoughtfully stocked with fashion-forward and cult lines, such as
Cheap Monday, Something Else by Natalie Wood, RetroSuperFuture and more.

Photos by Tracey Ayton Photography

Cara and Lauren Stryer

Q&A

What tip would you give women
who are starting a business?
It will take a lot of planning, research and,
more than anything, a whole lot of love and
passion for the project you are building!

Who is your role model or mentor?
We grew up in our parents' antique store,
watching them build and run their own business.
This really instilled a strong work ethic in
us and planted the entrepreneurial spirit.

What motivates you on a daily basis?
We are constantly motivated by each other's
ideas and the everyday growth of our business.

What do you CRAVE?
Good clothes, good music, good
food and good company!

VITAMINDAILY.COM

vitamindaily.com, Twitter: @vanvitamindaily

Irreverent. Trustworthy. Trendsetting.
VitaminDaily.com is a free online magazine that dispenses "style vitamins" that
help women get the most out of their city. Daily Doses have timely tips like a
new raw food café, eco-dry cleaner, custom-made shoes, or the best bakery for
macaroons. Launched in Vancouver in 2004, the site now has 6 editions across
Canada, an all-female staff of 15 and publishes half a million newsletters monthly.

Sarah Bancroft and
Tara Parker Tait

Q&A

What are your most popular products or services?
Our Editors' Diary blog shows funny, behind-the-scenes footage of our editors as they test products, attend glam launches, interview celebrities and prowl the streets for the best undiscovered scoops.

Who is your role model or mentor?
Natalie Massenet of Net-a-Porter.com— the definition of grace and ambition.

What motivates you on a daily basis?
We feel strongly about supporting other small businesses who don't have a big marketing war chest—exposure on our site can make a huge difference—we love to see that happen.

How do you relax?
We are both massage addicts. We often arrive at the office with lines all over our faces.

WALRUS

Caroline D. Boquist

 Q&A

What are your most popular products or services?
Lumen from Adam Frank, bird nests and houses by J. Shatz, chimpanzee candelabras by Seletti, jewellery by Broken English and our events that celebrate the local design community!

What tip would you give women who are starting a business?
Listen carefully, do your research, think critically and have a strong passion behind what you're doing. That passion needs to be big enough to carry you through it all!

What is your favourite part about owning a small business?
The creative freedom, meeting and collaborating with amazing individuals and the fulfilment of working for myself.

What is your motto or theme song?
Think with your heart, execute with your mind...

WALRUS

3408 Cambie St, Vancouver, 604.874.9770
walrushome.com, Twitter: @walrushome

Thoughtful. Collaborative. Whimsical.
Walrus is a contemporary home and gift shop that's sure to delight!
Whimsical yet functional designs line the shelves and tables in a
thoughtful and inviting way. While Walrus sources internationally,
they are also proud supporters of local creatives and showcase
their work by hosting evening events to celebrate.

Q&A

Zahra Mamdani

What tip would you give women who are starting a business?
Just do it, but with your eyes wide open. Know that it is going to take you more time and more money than you ever planned. But it's worth it!

What is your favourite part about owning a small business?
I get to see the smile on customers' faces when they find that fabulous item they were looking for—and I know I played a small part in that happiness.

Who is your role model or mentor?
Natalie Massenet! She has two kids and dove into Net-a-Porter without knowing anything about running a business.

WEAR ELSE

2360 W Fourth Ave, Vancouver, 604.732.3521
Park Royal Mall: 2015 Park Royal S, West Vancouver, 604.925.0058
Oakridge Mall: W 41st Ave, Vancouver, 604.266.3613
wearelse.com, Twitter: @WearElse

Cool. Trendy. Service-oriented.
Wear Else has been a premier destination for women's fashions for more
than 30 years. Since the company was acquired by its new owner, Zahra
Mamdani, in October 2007, a new vitality has been infused into the business.
Wear Else now offers the hottest brands of denim, T-shirts, attire, dresses
and more, while still offering lots of career options for the working girl.

Vivian Ko Gooch

Q&A

What is your favourite part about
owning a small business?
I have the freedom to be inventive and
creative in what I do best and therefore
the ability to be a chameleon.

Who is your role model or mentor?
It's always been my dad, Raymond—he taught
me to be compassionate, hard-working and
patient. I'm still learning to be a better listener!

What is your motto or theme song?
Risk must be taken because the greatest
hazard in life is to risk nothing at all.

What place inspires you and why?
Japan inspires me because of how the old world
meets new technology. Finding that modern
twist in some things so traditional or classic
every time you turn the corner is amazing.

WINK BEAUTY LOUNGE

67 E Cordova St, Vancouver, 604.696.9465
winkbeautylounge.com, Twitter: @winkbeauty

IN A WINK BEAUTIQUE

2627 Shaughnessy St, Port Coquitlam, 604.468.8113
inawinkbeautique.com, Twitter: @inawinkbeauty

Dynamic. Cheerful. Contemporary.
Wink Beauty Lounge, best known for semi-permanent eyelash extensions, is Vancouver's first open-concept spa boutique combining a premium retail cosmetic store blended with unique and classic spa services. The Wink Beauty Group Inc. has two locations in the Lower Mainland and offer classes and distribute Peepshow Lashes eyelash extension supplies to professionals in the Greater Vancouver area.

WISH.LIST BOUTIQUE

2811 W Broadway, Vancouver, 604.676.8070
wishlistboutique.ca, Twitter: @wishlistboutiqu

Trendy. Quality. Chic.
Wish.list boutique carries new-to-Vancouver designer lines of jewellery, handbags, beauty products, lingerie and more. The boutique features carefully selected designers, with an emphasis on the unusual. For the fashionista wanting LA chic meets pink and girly, wish.list has rockin' accessories, natural and organic makeup and beauty products, and one-of-a-kind gifts.

Photos by Sukh Gill-man Photography

Alisa and Kathie West Folk

 # Q&A

What is your favourite part about owning a small business?
Alisa: Shopping for others!
Kathie: Waking up every morning and coming to work in my own shop.

Who is your role model or mentor?
Alisa: Sarah Jessica Parker for her sense of style, independent spirit and talent.
Kathie: Stella McCartney as a socialite, fashionista and successful businesswoman.

What motivates you on a daily basis?
Each other! Our biggest motivation happens over a great dinner and a bottle of wine, discussing ideas for our boutique and future plans.

What is your motto or theme song?
"To succeed in life, you need three things: a wishbone, a backbone and a funnybone."—Reba McEntire

Jennifer Gallacher-Findlay

Q&A

What are your most popular products or services?
Local draught beer, made-from-scratch burgers, live entertainment and, of course, our perfectly poured pints of Guinness.

What tip would you give women who are starting a business?
Don't be scared to try something new and *always* trust your instincts. If you have passion and love what you do, the customers and the rewards will follow.

What is your favourite part about owning a small business?
Having the freedom to be my own boss, the ability to make all my creative ideas a reality and working side-by-side with my husband.

What do you CRAVE?
Balance in my life and Smartfood popcorn in my tummy.

THE WOLF & HOUND

3617 W Broadway, Vancouver, 604.738.8909
thewolfandhound.com, Twitter: @TheWolfAndHound

Cozy. Warm. Lively.
Located in the heart of Kitsilano, The Wolf & Hound is a favourite
among the locals for its service, food, award-winning beer selection,
live music and authentic atmosphere. Family-owned and operated,
the owners strive to make your experience as welcoming, comfortable
and relaxing as possible. In fact, it's so comfortable that many
customers call The Wolf & Hound their "home away from home."

WONDERBUCKS URBAN ALLEY

909 W Broadway, Vancouver, 604.742.0510
1803 Commercial Drive, Vancouver, 604.253.0510
wonderbucks.ca

Fun. Urban. New.
A Vancouver retail legend, Wonderbucks Urban Alley started as a retro general store 13 years ago and continues to "wow" and excite customers with edgy merchandise and apartment-sized furniture. This is "Let's go for lunch and shopping with the girls" kind of fun. Beware: it is addictive, and with retail prices up to 70 percent less than specialty stores, it is no longer "a secret in the city."

Frances Blazich with her daughter, Danica

Q&A

What are your most popular products or services?
Decorative accessories, furniture, pillows, kitchen, bath, art, plants and garden, all for your home.

What tip would you give women who are starting a business?
Start with your dream and develop it with your customers; you will need to reinvent yourself every 18 months.

Who is your role model or mentor?
Ann Angel, who mentored me in the fabric business as a young girl.

What place inspires you and why?
My home, because I am a homebody and love to dazzle myself in my safe place.

What motivates you on a daily basis?
My daughter, Danica.

ZING PAPERIE & DESIGN

60-323 Jervis St, Vancouver, 604.630.1885
zingdesign.ca, Twitter: @zingpaperie

Fresh. Modern. Chic.
Zing Paperie & Design, a bright and airy stationery boutique, is located on Vancouver's beautiful Coal Harbour seawall. This is your place to find designer cards, stylish paper goods, unique gifts, and other treasures that are sure to inspire. Zing also offers custom design services allowing one to order personalised paper couture. Look for Zing's online shop coming soon!

Q&A

Tiffany Barkman

What are your most popular
products or services?
Reusable fabric wraps, sleek magnetic
strips for stylish organization, page
flags, cute baby slippers, pocket travel
candles and custom-designed calling
cards for personal use or for business.

What tip would you give women
who are starting a business?
Love what you do and this will help carry you
through the hard work and challenges.

What is your favourite part about
owning a small business?
It's a creative outlet. I also love the flexibility
and autonomy. Yes, everything can land on
my shoulders, but for me, it's worth it.

Who is your role model or mentor?
I admire Sarah Richardson. She exudes passion
for her work, and I appreciate that she can
laugh at her own mistakes. We all make them!

ZOOLU ORGANICS

604.787.3571
zooluorganics.com, Twitter: @zooluorganics

Stylish. Sustainable. Modern.
Zoolu proves that organic doesn't have to mean boring, and children's clothing
doesn't have to be cliché or cutesy. Zoolu is for everyone who wants to buy
hip clothing with a conscience for the beloved babies and kids in their lives.

Photos by Bopomo Pictures

Patty Abbott

# Q&A

What are your most popular
products or services?
Right now, the short-sleeve onesies.

What tip would you give women
who are starting a business?
Do a lot of research and figure out what
makes you stand out from your competition.

What is your favourite part about
owning a small business?
I love the creative aspect of it all. I love design
and it's amazing to have the opportunity to
provide a product to consumers that I love.

How do you relax?
By spending time with my son, Raine.
His smile melts my heart.

What do you CRAVE?
Chai tea from the Granville Island Tea Company!

Kari Staten

Q&A

What are your most popular products or services?
Zuka's statement necklaces—always unique and on point for the new season's collections, charm bracelets (clients collect them), and one-on-one custom design for brides and their wedding parties.

What is your favourite part about owning a small business?
I enjoy the freedom of being my own boss, the flexibility of my work hours, and the fact that I'm doing something that makes me happy every day!

What is your motto or theme song?
My mission statement... To create with inspiration, to work with passion and to build with soul.

ZUKA ARTFUL ACCESSORIES

604.687.5747
zuka-art.com, Twitter: @zukaart

Romantic. Timeless. Unique.
Zuka draws from the emergence of what is meaningful with precious pieces
that have a history. From the ethereal elegance of turn-of-the-century pieces
to the earthiness of artisan-inspired treasures, Zuka is known for its beautiful
handmade jewellery which is produced in Vancouver using an eclectic mix
of stones, crystals and findings from all around the world. Zuka is found
in various high-end boutiques across Canada and the United States.

What place inspires you and why?

" *Vancouver inspires us. There are so many opportunities for women in this city, and we are proud to be among women who are making positive contributions to our community.* "

Katrina Carroll-Foster, Louise Kozier, Katie Schaeffers and Sarah Ueland of Y.E.S! Vancouver

Intelligentsia

Business-to-business entreprenesses, including coaching, marketing, and public relations, photography, business consulting, and design services.

Photos by Blue Olive Photography

AMY SAHOTA

778.232.4083
amysahota.blogspot.com, Twitter: @AmySahota

Determined. Confident. Engaging.
In the last four years, Amy Sahota has had a variety of media roles in both radio and television. You can find her working around the clock, always looking for people with an interesting story. If you want to know what goes on behind the scenes and meet local TV personalities and designers, follow Amy and she'll connect you to all the hot and exciting events in Vancouver.

Amy Sahota

Who is your role model or mentor?
I look up to women like Erin Cebula and Rena Heer. I love how their genuine personalities show on camera and how they are actively involved in the community.

What is your biggest fear?
Regretting that I never tried something I had a passion for, thus missing out on an opportunity.

What motivates you on a daily basis?
I am motivated by my passion to work hard because I believe it will get me to where I want to be next.

What is your motto or theme song?
"Be who you are and say what you feel because those who mind don't matter and those who matter don't mind."—Dr. Seuss

How do you relax?
I love being by the ocean in White Rock. Looking out into the water, it always feels like nothing is impossible or too big to happen.

What place inspires you and why?
Having friends around helps keep me positive and motivated to be a better person and inspires me to always want to do more and never settle for less.

What do you CRAVE?
I crave everyone feeling empowered to do what they want to do in life and feeling confident they can do anything if they set their minds to it.

Sarah
Morton

Q&A

What are your most popular products or services?
Outlook (which provides real-time email, calendar and contact synchronization from iPhones, BlackBerries and web browsers), our online data backup and QuickBooks, offered online anywhere.

What tip would you give women who are starting a business?
Definitely double and triple check your plan. Think everything through and know it will likely take longer than you think! Surround yourself with supportive, helpful people.

What is your favourite part about owning a small business?
My favourite part is being able to surround myself with a great team and great clients. I work with really interesting people every day.

What motivates you on a daily basis?
Opportunity. There is so much possibility in which to expand.

What place inspires you and why?
Getting out of the city inspires me. I love to come back to Vancouver but am always interested in seeing how other people live and the different paces of life.

BACKBONE SYSTEMS
AND NETWORKS CORP.

604.629.5538
backbonesystems.ca, Twitter: @backbonesystems

Geek-chic. Techno-friendly. Dynamic.
Backbone Systems takes the complication and confusion out of
technology and enables small businesses to use it in an easy and
affordable way to grow their business. Backbone houses and manages
all systems in their state-of-the-art data centre. Clients connect over
the Internet from anywhere to access their data and applications.

Q&A

What are your most popular products or services?
Transformational strategy days, customised individual coaching and group facilitation. Clients tend to rave about the strategy days as they are designed to break through blocks to their success.

What tip would you give women who are starting a business?
Do what makes your heart sing, believe in yourself and stay in action! Engage a coach for clarity and support, to inspire your momentum and to move through challenges effortlessly!

Who is your role model or mentor?
My father, who instilled in me a sense of higher purpose and a drive to succeed, and my mother, who taught me the importance of creating strong, genuine relationships.

What motivates you on a daily basis?
Making a difference with everyone I touch really fuels me, as well as a sense of accomplishment. A vanilla cupcake with coconut cream icing can also get me going.

What do you CRAVE?
My taste buds say artisan cheeses, a chilled glass of prosecco and a bowl full of crème brûlée. My heart says great conversation, making a difference and connected relationships.

Brita McLaughlin

BRITA MCLAUGHLIN COACHING

778.294.1429
britamclaughlincoaching.com, Twitter: @britamclaughlin

Empowering. Transformative. Solution-oriented.
Brita is an experienced certified life and relationship coach who equips
clients with knowledge, new perspectives, practical strategies and smart
relationship skills. Brita is passionate about helping working women
connect with the heart of who they are and raise the bar for themselves.
Brita believes that when a woman steps into her best self, she creates the
professional and personal success and fulfillment she's always wanted.

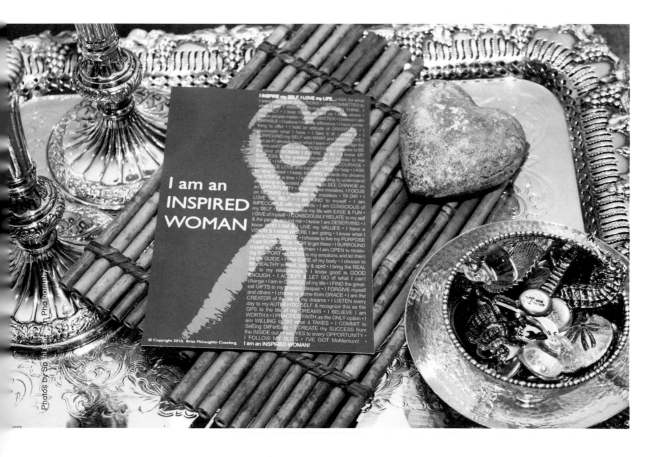

CHANGEMAKERS TOOLBOX

604.628.7902
changemakerstoolbox.com, Twitter: @lisaprincic

Inspiring. Compassionate. Savvy.
As a fully trained business coach, Lisa Princic works with changemakers, social entrepreneurs and green businesses to maximise their positive impact on the world while they do what they love. Her own personal quest to leave the "rat race," enjoy fulfilling work and live healthily has given her the tools to help others create successful businesses and meaningful change without compromising their lifestyles of freedom and balance.

Q&A

What are your most popular
products or services?
Most clients love the personal connection and
support they receive from one-on-one coaching,
although many gain invaluable benefits from the
synergy created in my Changemaker Business
Breakthrough group coaching program.

What tip would you give women
who are starting a business?
Don't wait until you are "ready," just do it!
The willingness to explore and take risks
is essential in order to figure out your
best path to success and happiness.

What is your favourite part about
owning a small business?
I love the creativity to reinvent myself
and my offerings to fit the needs of my
clients and my own passion to contribute.
The possibilities are truly infinite!

What motivates you on a daily basis?
I get a big high from helping others achieve
their own sense of accomplishment and
happiness. Making a living empowering others
to be fully alive and fulfilled is incredible!

What place inspires you and why?
Hiking and biking in the mountains and
travelling anywhere provide me with
perspective, renewed energy, and remind
me of what is most important in life:
adventure, connection and presence.

Lisa Princic

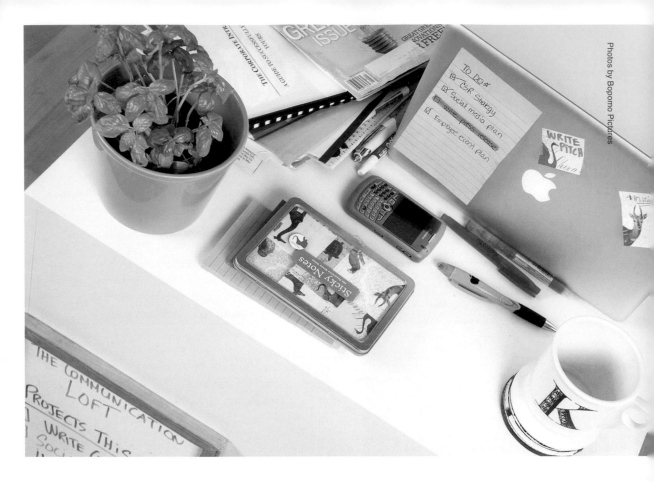

THE COMMUNICATION LOFT

communicationloft.ca, Twitter: @commsloft

Honest. Creative. Strategic.

The Communication Loft is an intimate, full-service communications agency specialising in public relations, media training, communications strategy and professional writing. Aiming to help small Vancouver businesses reach big heights, Kelly Aldinger takes pride in offering a uniquely creative approach to every client and every project. From the downright quirky to the straight-up traditional, she works to help each individual client's goals and objectives.

Kelly Aldinger

Q&A

What are your most popular products or services?
Integrated media programs—an approach that fuses traditional editorial media relations with the latest social media strategies. Helping other small businesses write creative copy is also a big one.

What tip would you give women who are starting a business?
Celebrate the small victories. Your first client, your first compliment, your first pay cheque—it's important to take time out from the bustle to breathe and smile.

What is your favourite part about owning a small business?
For me, it's the flexibility. Some days, I work really long hours, but there are also slower days when I can take an afternoon off and play a little!

Who is your role model or mentor?
Since I was little I've idolized John Lennon. He was a poet who fought for what he believed and walked his own path in life without worrying what others thought.

What motivates you on a daily basis?
Happiness. There's something really addictive about being excited to wake up every day. I've only truly felt that way since I branched out on my own.

The Communication Loft

The Communication Loft is a full-service communications strategy and public service markets.

With a flare for the creative & an instinct for reach big heights through editorial coverage targeted audiences.

The Tool Closet
In true loft style, we believe with less of an impact or here's a peek insid

DAYNA HOLLAND & ASSOCIATES LTD.

778.838.6929
daynahollandtax.com

Collaborative. Strategic. Down-to-earth.
Dayna Holland & Associates Ltd. is a public accounting firm that specialises in small- to medium-sized businesses. Their objective is to help clients understand the current financial position of their business and assist them in getting to the next stage. Dayna Holland & Associates Ltd. provides services ranging from corporate income tax return preparation to budgeting workshops.

Dayna Holland

 # Q&A

What are your most popular
products or services?
Explaining corporate taxes and operational
tax issues, brainstorming/budget planning and
corporate income tax return preparation.

What tip would you give women
who are starting a business?
Numbers aren't the be-all and end-
all of your business, but once they are
understood, they can be a very effective
tool that can help your business grow.

Who is your role model or mentor?
My dad (Dan Nakagawa), Andy Telford and
Elizabeth Owens. All three have taught
me the most about being a chartered
accountant and how to believe in myself.

What motivates you on a daily basis?
Continuing to meet businesses that
are intimidated by numbers and
knowing that I can help them.

How do you relax?
Skiing, gym time, hanging out with my
family and a nice glass of red wine.

What do you CRAVE?
Balance, new adventures, and a happy family.

Q&A

What are your most popular products or services?
Virtual assistant and personal shopping services for small business owners and busy professionals.

What tip would you give women who are starting a business?
You know what you are good at, you know what makes you happy, so follow your gut and give it 100 percent.

What is your favourite part about owning a small business?
The variety of projects I get to work on and the flexibility to set my own schedule. In my particular business, the talent I'm surrounded with is pretty amazing!

What motivates you on a daily basis?
Being able to teach a client or reader something new, and the knowledge that I'm helping to make someone's day easier or business more profitable.

What is your motto or theme song?
Those who wish to sing will always find a song!

How do you relax?
Date night with my husband, walking my dog, baking, dinners with my best friends or floating on an air mattress on any warm BC lake.

Kristi Ferguson

DOUBLE YOU
BUSINESS SERVICES

778.298.4255
doubleyoubiz.com, Twitter: @doubleyoukristi

FRASER VALLEY PULSE

fraservalleypulse.com, Twitter: @fvpulse

Dynamic. Virtual. Collaborative.
Kristi Ferguson founded Double You Business Services in 2004. Initially launched as a virtual assistant service, the company profile has grown to include a bustling personal shopping division. Double You works with clients throughout Metro Vancouver, the Fraser Valley and across the globe. To share the local gems she has discovered, Kristi launched FraserValleyPulse.com, a lifestyle guide featuring entrepreneurial ventures and community events in BC's Fraser Valley.

Portrait by Go-Lucky Photography, main photo (this page) and upper left photo (opposite page) by Tracey Ayton Photography

Krishna Bhowmik

Q&A

What are your most popular products or services?
Killer idea generation and design using a non-traditional approach to advertising including digital, social media, print and brand identity. We help new and existing companies reveal their best potential.

What is your favourite part about owning a small business?
It's like kindergarten when you get a lump of Play-Doh and you can do whatever you want with it.

What is your motto or theme song?
"Eye of the Tiger."

What is your biggest fear?
Moving to a new office... in the alleyway!

What place inspires you and why?
Coffee shops. I like how they're filled with people from all walks of life. Sometimes I overhear conversations... okay, borderline eavesdrop, and there's great raw material there. People are entertaining.

What do you CRAVE?
A few more hands, heads, legs, a chef, a foot rub, a trip to Copenhagen and a Herman Miller chair.

⊙ FLEABARK
💡 ADVERTISING AND DESIGN

604.781.5505
fleabark.com, Twitter: @fleabark

Inventive. Adventurous. Meticulous.
Armed with remarkable ideas, Fleabark Advertising and Design are new, exciting, progressive idea generators for the 21st century. Their extraordinary creative thinking hails from an award-winning background of 12 years of international experience including Europe and the Middle East. They know how to move people, get them talking and create a buzz that spreads. You will be in exceptional hands.

Photos by Michael Chui Photography, except main photo (this page) by Johnny Lo Photography

FORUM FOR WOMEN ENTREPRENEURS (BC)

604.682.8115
fwe.ca, Twitter: @FWEBC

Fresh. Personal. Accessible.
Forum for Women Entrepreneurs (FWE) is a non-profit society for women entrepreneurs and entrepreneurial-minded professionals. Its mission is to mentor and educate women entrepreneurs through leading-edge professional programs and facilitate connections within the business community.
Since 2002, FWE has been creating a growing community; currently it's supporting members through eight programs and an annual gala.

Jill Earthy and Christina Anthony

Q&A

What are your most popular products or services?
The e-series Program, Mentor Program, a-series Program, Roundtables, Peer Advisory Circles, Member Forums, Student Internship, and k-series Program... and, of course, our annual gala is not to be missed!

What tip would you give women who are starting a business?
Surround yourself with people who support and inspire you. Find resources that can help you take your ideas to the next level. Don't be afraid to ask for help.

What motivates you on a daily basis?
We are motivated and inspired by the passion and determination of all women entrepreneurs and entrepreneurial-minded professionals. Their stories, opportunities, struggles and experiences—they are why we exist!

What place inspires you and why?
Our events. They are where connections are established and ideas take flight. The energy is always incredible. Plus, everyone dresses up, looks great and has fun!

What do you CRAVE?
Seeing women entrepreneurs take their businesses to the next level and witnessing collaboration among smart, savvy people. Success stories give us goose bumps!

Heather White and Felicia Lee

Q&A

What tip would you give women
who are starting a business?
Get clear on the benefits and/or solutions
that your business model is providing and
have a true understanding of the kind of niche
markets that are searching for those benefits.

What is your favourite part about
owning a small business?
Being in the driver's seat of our own
destiny. Having a business allows
the balance between personal and
professional life to blend seamlessly.

What motivates you on a daily basis?
Seeing the light bulb go on for the clients we
work with and therefore knowing we have
transferred knowledge, effectively giving
them new tools to grow their business.

What is your motto or theme song?
From a spark may burst a mighty flame.

How do you relax?
By spending time in nature, reconnecting
with ourselves through meditation and
spending time in or near the ocean.

What place inspires you and why?
The mouth of the ocean. It's vast,
open, inviting, mysterious, exciting
and calming all at the same time.

Had an idea...

As a global leader in business development and leadership skills for women, our various programs have been developed, delivered, and have achieved results for thousands of women across the globe.

www.GhostCEO.com

Vancouver - Seattle - San Francisco - Los Angeles - Miami - London

GHOST CEO ™

Vancouver - Seattle - San Francisco - LA - Miami - London

GHOST CEO

207-2628 Granville St, Vancouver, 604.833.3212
ghostceo.com, Twitter: @ghostceo

Proven. Guaranteed. Expert.
The Ghost CEO coaching program is a world-class business coaching and training program targeting entrepreneurs, working professionals, companies and organizations. Ghost CEO focuses entirely on business development, systems and other programming that support the expansion and profitability of a business in a sustainable model. Clients range from business start-ups to senior levels of management in Fortune 500 companies.

Q&A

What is your favourite part about owning a small business?
The flexibility and lifestyle. Achieving goals we never thought possible and celebrating the hell out of it!

Who is your role model or mentor?
All the amazing female entrepreneurs and businesswomen out there!

What motivates you on a daily basis?
We met over a love of champagne. Now best friends and business partners, we regroup every Friday for champagne lunch—what better motivator is there than that?

How do you relax?
Travel, spas, massages and Friday afternoon lunches on a sunny patio.

What place inspires you and why?
Kits Beach where we take walks, have partnership meetings, relax, exercise and refocus on our business and friendship. It reminds us how big the world is and how much there is to conquer and savour!

What do you CRAVE?
The fabulous group of power women at Jive and the energy we create and fiestiness with which we conquer the world. And champagne and a killer pair of heels!

Almira Bardai and
Lindsay Nahmiache

◉ JIVE COMMUNICATIONS

2610-131 Regiment Square, Vancouver, 604.568.7214
jivecommunications.ca

Fresh. Feisty. Fabulous.
Boutique PR agency Jive Communications' public relations services
combine strong strategic and creative management to deliver results
that consistently exceed expectations. Using fully integrated and
comprehensive PR and communications campaigns, Jive gets your
messages, stories and news to the media and the public through traditional
media relations, online media relations and targeted outreach.

Photos by Blue Olive Photography

Dream Designs photographed by Jordana Dhahan
of Through the Looking Glass Photography

What motivates you on a daily basis?

"Waking up every day with a fresh new start... creative ideas, networking groups, women in business and culture!"

Julia Linford of J Spa

L2 ACCENT REDUCTION CENTRE

6093 West Blvd, Vancouver, 604.267.7781
L2accent.com, Twitter: @jenmadigan

Life-changing. Confidence-building. Euphoric.
Don't let a heavy accent be a barrier in your workplace. L2 Accent Reduction Centre is a unique service that helps internationally trained professionals speak clearer and relate better by retraining the muscles of the mouth. Services are offered both locally and worldwide. The L2 Accent Reduction Centre has become a leader in working with global companies that have a diverse work force.

Q&A

What are your most popular products or services?
Our most popular services for individuals are the online courses because they allow for study on their own time.

What is your favourite part about owning a small business?
I love the creative aspect of business. It is something spectacular when you can take a creative concept and watch it actually come to life in the form of business.

Who is your role model or mentor?
My sister, Lisa, who has inspired me to start the Fresh Start Program, which offers our courses for free to all single immigrant parents.

What is your motto or theme song?
Work with corporations, do community work and offer your services to those who cannot afford it. Only then will you find harmony in your business.

How do you relax?
I like to make up songs on my guitar or banjo. (Though I can't really play either one.)

What place inspires you and why?
I love the woods, especially after it rains. It helps to clear my head and remember that there is so much abundance and joy in living.

Jennifer Madigan

Kerrisdale

Isabelle Mercier-Turcotte
and Margarita Romano

Q&A

What are your most popular
products or services?
Strategic planning, performance
coaching, brand revitalizations, The
Spark™ and LeapTV.com.

What tip would you give women
who are starting a business?
Get clear on what you want. Design your
business model to suit your ideal lifestyle.
Follow your gut and learn to say "No!"

Who is your role model or mentor?
Renée Safrata, our business coach. She truly
inspires us to live, love and keep it light.

What motivates you on a daily basis?
The satisfaction of getting things
done and done well.

What is your motto or theme song?
It's better to do it than to dwell on it.

How do you relax?
Daily yoga and meditation, doggy walks,
dinner with friends and movie nights.

What place inspires you and why?
Chapters Bookstores. Perusing the
aisles is a great way to get juiced and to
problem solve just about anything.

What do you CRAVE?
Travelling—learning, exploring and just being.

LEAPZONE
STRATEGIES

604.312.9613
leapzonestrategies.com, Twitter: @leapzone

Simple. Momentum-generating. Bold.
LeapZone Strategies helps committed entrepreneurs get clear on their
brand, raise the bar and align their business, team and communications
to create a consistent experience for their customers; thereby increasing
company credibility, profitability and most importantly, customer trust through
business strategies, performance coaching and brand alignment.

Sandra Garcia

Q&A

What are your most popular products or services?
Most people come to me to get exposure in the media, but more recently I've been asked to help others with business writing and editing.

What tip would you give women who are starting a business?
Don't be afraid to get your feet wet. Be clear on who your audience is, and make sure what you're doing will make you money!

Who is your role model or mentor?
My older sister is my role model. She's already accomplished so much at a young age, and is just getting started.

What motivates you on a daily basis?
The fact that my work helps others reach their business goals and sometimes helps to fulfill great philanthropic causes. My business ends when it stops helping others.

What is your motto or theme song?
"Small company, BIG results!" I also love what a character in the movie *Jerry Maguire* says: "Roll with the punches, tomorrow's another day."

What place inspires you and why?
I love being in downtown Vancouver because it always feels like there's something going on, whether it's work, a cultural event, a party, or just people trying to get somewhere.

◎ MIDDLE CHILD MARKETING

604.721.0030
middlechildmarketing.com, Twitter: @mc_marketing

Goal-oriented. Independent. Fun.
Sandra Garcia is the owner, publicist and public relations consultant for Middle Child Marketing. Capitalizing on the proverbial "middle child syndrome" and how it relates to business marketing, Sandra uses her knowledge and expertise of public relations to communicate stories about events and businesses to the media and online audiences. Middle Child Marketing serves businesses in entertainment, fashion and beauty.

OMGWTF CREATIVE

778.938.3150
omgwtfcreative.com, Twitter: @omgwtfcreative

Unique. Powerful. Innovative.
OMGWTF Creative is a social media marketing company that works with
a variety of businesses and individuals to increase their online presence
through social networking sites. Not only does OMGWTF provide creative
services by creating one-of-a-kind social networking pages such as custom
Facebook tabs, but it also acts as a personal "social networking assistant"
posting your company's updates online and tweeting to the world!

Photos by Blue Olive Photography

Q&A

Whitney Krutzfeldt

What are your most popular
products or services?
Custom Facebook tabs and "Social Networking
Assistant" packages; everyone loves the idea
of not having to be on Facebook, Twitter or
blogs all day and that's where we come in!

What is your favourite part about
owning a small business?
Being able to connect with businesses on a
personal level. I get to see all of the results
firsthand and be proud of the work I've done.

Who is your role model or mentor?
My mom is the most remarkable, hard
working woman; she has always been
an amazing role model to me.

How do you relax?
Photography. Travel. Friends.
Good food and wine!

What place inspires you and why?
What really inspires me are my friends.
I've been truly lucky to be surrounded by
people who are passionate about life and
that's what pushes me to be successful.

What do you CRAVE?
I crave travel! I love being excited about
experiencing something new, and knowing
that I'm going to meet unforgettable people
and see some really amazing things!

Elizabeth J. Mah

Yours truly,
Elizabeth J. Mah

Q&A

What is your favourite part about
owning a small business?
I learn something about myself every day.
Owning a business forces me to reflect on
my values and priorities and to cultivate an
inner strength to stand firmly by them.

Who is your role model or mentor?
My dad. He's wise and principled, caring
and protective (sometimes overly) but
most importantly, always a teacher
and supportive of who I am.

What is your biggest fear?
Losing confidence in my gut feeling,
my potential and my capability.

What motivates you on a daily basis?
Making sure I live my life without regrets.
Being able to look back and say that I
faced and conquered each challenge.

What is your motto or theme song?
"Jump and grow wings on the way
down." Every decision has its risks and
obstacles, and although I will be bruised
along the way, I will make it great!

How do you relax?
A visit to my acupuncturist and RMT, laughing
uncontrollably until my tummy hurts with my
mom and sister, and then having a glass of
Riesling on the patio with my husband.

POGODA STUDIO

604.613.9474
pogodastudio.com, Twitter: @Joanna__Moss

Creative. Modern. Poised.
Pogoda Studio is a boutique-style graphic and website design studio,
specialising in working with small- to mid-size businesses and start-ups.
Offering comprehensive design services from a simple business card to
a complete corporate identity, they work with clients from concept straight
through to implementation and print. Pogoda Studio is dedicated to providing
customers with the highest level of service, support and jargon-free advice.

Joanna Moss

⬛ Q&A

**What tip would you give women
who are starting a business?**
Don't give up! Don't get discouraged when
it gets tough, surround yourself by other
successful women and learn from them.

**What is your favourite part about
owning a small business?**
The ability to try new things, implement
new ideas and services, and the flexibility
to have a career and be a full-time mom.

Who is your role model or mentor?
My mother. She always encouraged my
creativity; she still has artwork I made
for her in school. I get my determination,
passion and drive to succeed from her.

What motivates you on a daily basis?
My son. I want to show him that if
you set attainable goals for yourself,
you can accomplish big things.

What is your motto or theme song?
Harder, Better, Faster, Stronger by Daft Punk.

How do you relax?
A mani-pedi is the best way
to relax and regroup.

What do you CRAVE?
I crave success and shoes. I think
they go hand in hand; success means
shoe shopping as a reward.

Q & A

Natasha Raey

What are your most popular products or services?
Business development, strategic planning, marketing/public relations program evaluation, event planning, community-based research, team building/organizational development, plain language communication and training.

What tip would you give women who are starting a business?
Be courageous and creative. Set goals and make a plan to help you achieve those goals. Be authentic, honest and willing to embrace lifelong learning. Network, network, network!

What is your favourite part about owning a small business?
The flexibility to pick projects that fit my interests. Being able to help small businesses with my skills and expertise and working with a range of diverse organizations.

What motivates you on a daily basis?
Making a difference. I am motivated by being able to help move projects and organizations forward so that they can reach their full potential.

What place inspires you and why?
Anywhere near the water—the serenity puts me at ease and gets me to my most creative place.

RAEY CONSULTING

778.552.4538
raeyconsulting.com, Twitter: @RaeyConsulting

Creative. Fresh. Innovative.
Raey Consulting prides themselves on being expressive, empathetic
communicators with proven experience working with diverse groups.
They have worked in the non-profit, municipal and small business sectors
extensively and are comfortable in situations that require resourceful
thinking outside the box and a creative approach to problem solving.

REX IMAGE

715-938 Howe St, Vancouver, 604.628.4419
reximage.com, Twitter: @allisoncousins

Fresh. Authentic. Versatile.
When retailers, real estate developers, consultants, service providers,
and visionaries want to *get a response* from a new audience—a bigger
audience, a better audience—they call Rex Image, a marketing and design
agency with an unscripted and authentic approach to marketing and
the client relationship, since 2005. You've seen their work around town
in newsprint, online, on bus shelters and transit, video and more.

Allison J. Cousins

Q&A

What is your favourite part about owning a small business?
My #1 value is relationship. Through business ownership I have the opportunity to create space for my personal relationships and to choose awesome clients and colleagues.

What is your biggest fear?
Giving up too soon and missing out. I never want to leave a stone unturned—I'm doggedly committed to anything I set my mind to. That and the dark.

What motivates you on a daily basis?
I can't explain it other than to say I have a deep, internal desire to feel I've done my very best.

What is your motto or theme song?
Say yes to anything that will enrich my life experience.

What place inspires you and why?
There is a little town in Mexico called Ajijic. It's inland and far from the tourist beaches. When I'm there, surrounded by the community-minded culture, possibilities expand.

What do you CRAVE?
I crave growth. I love experiencing it personally, and I love being around it or a part of it when someone I care about is growing.

SOYA MARKETING

604.568.5405
soyamarketing.com, Twitter: @soya_marketing

Helpful. Inventive. Curious.
Soya Marketing helps companies get their stories to the market using the
art of web storytelling. Soya has worked with Pacific Centre, Park Royal, BC
Medical Association and the 2009 World Police & Fire Games. Co-founders
Debbie and Jacqueline believe in the power of stories to connect people.
They aim to make social media simple for companies to use.

Q&A

What are your most popular products or services?
Our three-step program, The Soya System. It's a fast, easy way for companies to get their stories out on Google, Facebook, Twitter, YouTube and all across the web.

What tip would you give women who are starting a business?
Deb: Maintain balance. If you don't take time for yourself, you can easily lose focus.
Jacqueline: Seek advice from the get-go. Talk to business owners who know their stuff.

What is your favourite part about owning a small business?
Deb: The constant learning and discovery. It's the most rewarding thing I have done so far.
Jacqueline: Being a business owner is being an inventor. It's an act of creation.

Who is your role model or mentor?
Many remarkable people we've met through the Forum for Women Entrepreneurs.

How do you relax?
Deb: Yoga and spending time with friends.
Jacqueline: Music, meditation and Pilates.

What do you CRAVE?
Deb: Weekends off and yummy food.
Jacqueline: A constant flow of great experiences.

Debbie Collins and
Jacqueline Voci

Q&A

Darci LaRocque

What tip would you give women
who are starting a business?
Never underestimate yourself, and take
chances. Always remember that there are
no failures, only lessons to be learned.

What is your favourite part about
owning a small business?
The delight of seeing your business
grow and flourish is a real high. Being
your own boss gives you freedom—
freedom to succeed, as well as fail.

What is your biggest fear?
Although I pride myself on keeping on
top of projects, there's always a fear
that there won't be enough hours in the
day. This helps keep me sharp!

What motivates you on a daily basis?
Making our training workshops engaging and
fun. I *always* want our clients to walk away
saying "That was the best training session *ever!*"

What place inspires you and why?
Anywhere with a spectacular view, which means
anywhere in Vancouver. What a place to live!

What do you CRAVE?
I crave a future when more people will
find technology fun and empowering.
Swirl Solutions is making that happen!

SWIRL SOLUTIONS

604.628.0284
swirlsolutions.com, Twitter: @swirlsolutions

Fun. Educational. Interactive.
Swirl Solutions is a BlackBerry Smartphone training company offering services worldwide. Swirl Solutions shows companies how staff can spend more time on their jobs through efficient use of technology. Wielding the technology the right way can save four hours a week and up to 40 percent on your wireless bills! Owner Darci is featured offering BlackBerry tips on GetConnected TV and in various publications.

Photos by Blue Olive Photography

Main photo (this page) by Amanda Buzard, portrait by Anastasia Photography

WHITEHOTTRUTH.COM

whitehottruth.com, Twitter: @daniellelaporte

Inspiring. Pragmatic. Authentic.

A recent list of the Top 10 Blogs by Women [That] Might Change Your Life describes Danielle and her blog: "She's confidently contrarian, feminine, decisive, creative. She combines spirituality with sound business... She has an e-program (Fire Starter Sessions) [for entrepreneurs]... and gives coaching sessions at $500 a pop. She's been listed, ranked and quoted... and is quite possibly the most talented and insightful writer publishing on the web."

Danielle LaPorte

Q&A

What are your most popular products or services?
The Fire Starter Sessions: A Digital Experience for Entrepreneurs. Spark Your Genius. Make It Matter. A percentage of sales from the book benefit the Acumen Fund or Women International. 1-on-1 Consults offer innovation and intuition focused on your work in the world.

What tip would you give women who are starting a business?
Get clear on how you really want to "feel" in your business. Once you know the desired feelings driving you, you can build a make-it-happen strategy that's magnetic.

What do you CRAVE?
Wide open spaces. Pineapple. Simplicity.

What motivates you on a daily basis?
I have a note on my laptop: MAKE STUFF. Make art. Make visions real. Make myself really, really useful. I'm motivated to go deeper into big life questions, and to make that inquiry my service to the world. It's pretty simple, actually: live (fully, deeply, lightly). Speak. Write... make stuff.

What is your motto or theme song?
Everything is progress. Everything.

What place inspires you and why?
Anywhere an authentic conversation is happening. Sincere curiosity, deep listening— truly interested people are inspiring. That, and Santa Fe at night, with the coyotes howling.

Katrina Carroll-Foster and
Louise Kozier (Co-Founders)
with Katie Schaeffers and
Sarah Ueland (Co-Chairs)

Q&A

What are your most popular
products or services?
Y.E.S! is where business and philanthropy meet
in style. Our monthly cocktail minglers and
signature events hosted at the trendiest venues
attract Vancouver's top female professionals.

Who is your role model or mentor?
Our role models are the inspirational, resilient
women who participate in the Dress for
Success programs as well as the fabulous
entrepreneurs with whom we share this guide!

What motivates you on a daily basis?
We are driven by our desire to support
disadvantaged women in our community
while creating opportunities for professional
development and making positive
connections with like-minded women.

How do you relax?
We work hard and play hard. Whether
we're building our business or climbing
the corporate ladder, a cocktail or yoga
session with Y.E.S! helps us relax in style.

What place inspires you and why?
Vancouver inspires us. There are so many
opportunities for women in this city, and we are
proud to be among women who are making
positive contributions to our community.

Y.E.S! VANCOUVER

604.408.7923
yesvancouver.org, Twitter: @YESVancouver

Fun. Meaningful. Engaging.
Y.E.S! Vancouver offers a fresh approach to networking and fundraising.
Connect with professional, friendly, stylish women at signature networking
events. Stay on top of what's hot in Vancouver while connecting with
Y.E.S! members and raising money to support Dress for Success.
Y.E.S! wishes to thank Blake, Cassels & Graydon LLP for supporting
their inclusion in the third edition of the CRAVE Vancouver Guide.

337

Icon Key

Featured Entreprenesses

 Abode Furniture, home improvement and interior design

 Adorn Jewellery, eyewear, handbags and accessories

 Connect Networking, media, technology and event services

 Details Gifts, books, small home accessories, florists and stationery

 Enhance Beauty, wellness, spas and fitness

 Escape Entertainment, travel and leisure activities

 Nurture Goods and services for babies, children and parents

 Pets Goods and services for pets and their owners

 Sip Savour Food and drink

 Style Clothing, shoes and stylists

Intelligentsia

 Coach Coaches and consultants

 Communicate Marketing, PR and branding strategy

 Create Graphic and web design and media services

 Entertain Event services

 Finance Accountants and money management specialists

 Law Law offices and attorneys

 Network Networking events, programs and social media

 Real Estate Real estate, property management and moving services

 Staff Staffing agencies and recruiters

 Support Organization services and personal assistants

 Tech Technology support

Additional

Nonprofit Not-for-profit business

Sustainable Devoted to environmentally friendly practices

Featured Entreprenesses by Category

Featured Entreprenesses by Category (continued)

Featured Entreprenesses by Category (continued)

Intelligentsia by Category

manifes

Entreprenesses by Neighbourhood

Entreprenesses by Neighbourhood (continued)

Entreprenesses by Neighbourhood (continued)

Contributors

At CRAVE Vancouver we believe in acknowledging, celebrating and passionately supporting locally owned businesses and entrepreneurs. We are extremely grateful to all contributors for this publication.

Albach Studios
photographer
888.456.7448
albachstudios.com
Twitter: @ALBACHfoto

Albach Studios specialises in people, product and food photography. Because there are no templates, text-book lighting schemes or studio backdrops (unless requested), Albach Studios creates authentic and original images.

Alison Turner
graphic designer
alisonjturner.com

Alison is a graphic designer, seamstress and block printer from Seattle, who supports human rights and the local food movement. In her spare time she enjoys music, cooking and being outside.

Amanda Buzard
editor and lead designer
amandabuzard.com

Amanda is a Seattle-based designer inspired by clean patterns and vintage design. She chases many creative and active pursuits in her spare time. Passions include Northwest travel, photography, dining out and creating community.

Blue Olive Photography
photographer
blueolivephotography.com

Blue Olive Photography is the boutique Vancouver-based wedding and portrait photography studio led by husband and wife photographers Reilly and Miranda Lievers. With a passion for sassy, unique images, these two love what they do and it shows!

Bopomo Pictures
photographer
604.678.1411, bopomo.ca
Twitter: @bopomopictures

Bopomo Pictures combines fun and affordability with quality photography in a hip studio setting. Bopomo creates timeless memories with maternity, baby and family pics, and helps professionals and businesses make a lasting impact with head shot and commercial photography.

Carrie Wicks
proofreader and copy editor
linkedin.com/in/carriewicks

Carrie has been proofreading professionally for 14-plus years in mostly creative fields. When she's not proofreading or copyediting, she's reading, singing jazz, walking in the woods or gardening.

Contributors

Crystal Chu
intern
crystal@craveparty.com

Crystal is currently a junior studying commerce at the University of British Columbia. She is actively involved in the Young Women in Business Network and aspires to be a successful entrepreness.

Go-Lucky Photography
photographer
778.245.3686, goluckyphoto.com
Twitter: @GoLuckyPhoto

Andrea Warner is the owner and lead photographer of Go-Lucky Photography. She holds her bachelor's degree in photography from the Emily Carr University and specialises in weddings and lifestyle portraiture.

Lilla Kovacs
operations manager
lilla@thecravecompany.com

Lilla has been with CRAVE since 2005. As the operations manager, she ensures that everything runs like clockwork. She loves shoe shopping, traveling, art and her MacBook.

Melissa Gidney Photography
photographer
778.388.8805, mgimages.ca
melissagidneyblog.com

Inspired by the moments in between and the simple things we overlook, Melissa strives to capture and create the memories that will last a lifetime. Fashion, art, weddings... life.

Mina Kim
intern
mina@craveparty.com

Mina is studying business in her third year at the University of British Columbia. She is part of the Young Women in Business Internship Program and has been actively involved with the Commerce Undergraduate Society.

Nicole Shema
project manager
nicole@thecravecompany.com

A Seattle native, Nicole is happy to be back in her city after graduating from the University of Oregon in 2009. Nicole has a passion for travel and loves discovering new places around Seattle with friends, running, shopping and reading in coffee shops.

Ronak Samadi
editorial contributor
ronak@craveparty.com

Ronak is a senior at the University of British Columbia. When she's not working or studying, she enjoys travelling and the outdoors. Her passions include art, philanthropy and, of course, shopping!

Sidney Ann Field
graphic designer
sidneyann.com

Sidney is a designer, crafter, seamstress, yogi and aspiring circus superstar. In her free time she can be found exploring Seattle's restaurant scene and spending time with her nieces and nephews.

Sukhi Ghuman Photography
photographer
sukhighuman.ca

Sukhi Ghuman is a Vancouver-based photographer specialising in documentary wedding, lifestyle and commercial photography. Bold colour, brilliant light and passionate personalities are the makeup of her legendary images.

Through the Looking Glass Photography
photographer
778.861.0543
jordana@lookingglass.biz

Jordana Dhahan specialises in commercial, portrait and travel photography. She believes photography is both the cause and result of looking for beauty, interest and uniqueness in everything. She's also a municipal and personal injury lawyer at spraggslaw.ca.

Tracey Ayton Photography
photographer
604.738.5605, tphotography.ca

With more than 15 years of experience in the photography business, Tracey Ayton has created her own beautiful style, which is reflected in the pictures she takes.

Additional thanks to Anna Stoll.

About Our Company

The CRAVE company innovatively connects small business owners with the customers they crave. We bring together small business communities and fuel them with entrepreneurial know-how and fresh ideas—from business consulting to shopping fairs to new media. The CRAVE company knows what it takes to thrive in the modern marketplace. To find out more about CRAVE in your city, visit thecravecompany.com.

CRAVEparty®

What Do You Crave?
CRAVEparty is an exclusive, festive, glam-gal gathering of fun, entertainment, personal pampering, specialty shopping, sippin' and noshin', and just hanging with the girls.

CRAVE guides™

Style and Substance. Delivered.
CRAVEguides are the go-to resource for urban-minded women. We celebrate stylish entrepreneurs by showcasing the gutsiest, most creative and interesting proprietors from cities all over the world.

CRAVE business™

A Fresh Approach to Modern Business.
CRAVEbusiness is all about making connections and sharing innovation. Our community is a diverse group of stylish, exciting and driven entrepreneurs, and we create all kinds of ways for you to connect with each other.

about

Craving Savings

Get the savings you crave with the following
participating entreprenesses—one time only!

10 percent off

- [ ] 18KARAT
- [ ] Absolute Confidence
- [ ] Babs Studio Boutique
- [ ] Bandidas Taquería
- [ ] The Bar Method
- [ ] Belmondo Organic Skin Care
- [ ] Bodacious Lifestyles Inc.
- [ ] Body politic
- [ ] Bombay Brow Bar
- [ ] Bow wow haus
- [ ] Brooklyn Designs
- [ ] Burke&Hair
- [ ] Carrington Shoppe, The
- [ ] Changes Clothing & Jewellery Bar
- [ ] Christa Leigh
- [ ] The Communication Loft
- [ ] Dream Designs
- [ ] Dutch Girl Chocolates
- [ ] Ecocessories
- [ ] Excentric Salon
- [ ] Feel Fabulous Mobile Spa
- [ ] Filou Designs
- [ ] Fine Finds
- [ ] Gentille Alouette
- [ ] High Heel Appeal
- [ ] Holly
- [ ] In A Wink Beautique
- [ ] Invito Couture
- [ ] ISHARA
- [ ] It's Your Move
- [ ] J spa
- [ ] Jag Dhahan
- [ ] Julie Tidiman, REALTOR®

10 percent off (continued)

- [ ] LAKSHMI
- [ ] LeapZone Strategies
- [ ] Lunapads International
- [ ] Luxe Beauty Lounge & Mobile Spa
- [ ] Maza Interior Design
- [ ] Mizuna Culinary
- [ ] My Edible Advice
- [ ] Nina Pousette
- [ ] Operation Style
- [ ] OWN THE ROOM
- [ ] Paperclip Law Corporation
- [ ] Pebble
- [ ] Raey Consulting
- [ ] Simply French Cafe
- [ ] Skindulgence
- [ ] Swirl Solutions
- [ ] Vincent Park
- [ ] Walrus
- [ ] Wear Else

20 percent off

- [ ] A Good Chick To Know
- [ ] BeautyInk Gallery
- [ ] Bella Ceramica
- [ ] Bodacious Life and Sex Coaching
- [ ] Bonn Chiropractic
- [ ] Changemakers Toolbox
- [ ] Della Optique
- [ ] Favourite Gifts
- [ ] Frankies Candy Bar
- [ ] Hagensborg Chocolates
- [ ] Jo's Toes & Esthetics

Craving Savings

20 percent off (continued)
- [ ] Lüt Boutique
- [ ] LYNNsteven Boutique
- [ ] OhKuol
- [ ] Peekaboo Beans
- [ ] Rouge Make-Up Lounge
- [ ] Sabai Thai Spa
- [ ] The Smarty Pants Gift Company Ltd.
- [ ] Spa Boutique
- [ ] Stripped Wax Bar
- [ ] Superfly Lullabies
- [ ] UrbanMommies
- [ ] Verve Hair Lounge
- [ ] Wink Beauty Lounge
- [ ] Wish.list boutique
- [ ] Wonderbucks Urban Alley
- [ ] Y.E.S! Vancouver
- [ ] Zing Paperie & Design
- [ ] Zuka Artful Accessories

30 percent off
- [ ] Barefoot Contessa
- [ ] Brita McLaughlin Coaching
- [ ] Elements Mineral Makeup
- [ ] Is. Salon
- [ ] Jericho Counselling Services
- [ ] Le Petit Spa
- [ ] Lusso Baby
- [ ] Pogoda Studio
- [ ] She to Shic Boutique Beauty Lounge
- [ ] SKN Holistic Rejuvenation Clinic
- [ ] Tracey Ayton Photography
- [ ] Tutta Mia
- [ ] VitaminDaily.com
- [ ] Zoolu Organics

50 percent off
- [ ] Urban Body Laser

Use code CRAVE for online discount if applicable.